Black & White Model Photography

Techniques & Images

Bill Lemon

Amherst Media ■ Buffalo, NY

Published by:
Amherst Media, Inc.
P.O. Box 586
Buffalo, N.Y. 14226
Fax: 716-874-4508

Publisher: Craig Alesse
Senior Editor/Project Manager: Richard Lynch
Associate Editor: Michelle Perkins
Image Technician: John Gryta

ISBN: 0-936262-68-0
Library of Congress Card Catalog Number: 98-70349

Printed in the United States of America.
10 9 8 7 6 5 4 3 2

Acknowledgements:
I would like to thank the models who made this book come to life, and helped make my dream come true. To name just a few: Dale Coleman, Annette McKnight, Kirsten Bucheister, Kirsten Harrison, Brandi Clymer and Franki Di. Thanks also go to Leslie Lemon and Cindy Lemon, my two daughters, who put up with a lot, but through all the mess encouraged me to keep with it. A special thanks to Vivienne Duff, who got me started in the wonderful world of photography with the gift of my first camera. A big thanks to Craig Alesse, the publisher, and Michelle Perkins, the editor, for all their help in making this book possible. Thanks also to Gary Frankel for all his creative printing, and to all the other labs that helped me with printing in this book. Finally, a huge thanks to the people of 'Studio 15 Workshop' for all their encouragement.

Introduction

Working image by image through sixty photographs, Bill Lemon reveals the technical and compositional techniques integral to his dramatic and sensual style of model photography. Posing examples cover a variety of techniques such as how to create the appearance of longer and slimmer legs, or tips for making breasts look their best. Examples and diagrams illustrate artificial lighting techniques for both indoor and outdoor settings, and helpful advice for using sunlight to create soft, natural effects. Photographic examples illustrate the importance of setting and composition, as well as how to make the most of every model's assets, whether shooting nude, semi-nude, or clothed images.

The volume explores a variety of photographic situations and shows how to respond to the challenges as a photographer. These include outdoor and studio settings, direct sunlight and shade, the inclusion of water and landscape elements, the use of props, the selection of clothing for black and white images, and the use of creative camera angles. Techniques for setting moods with lighting, props and poses are also covered.

After nearly two decades of working with models, Bill Lemon is a well qualified source of advice for identifying and establishing a professional relationship with models (professional or amateur) who fit your style. He details the importance of creating a comfortable and relaxed environment when working with models, and provides practical tips for helping nervous amateur models to look at ease in front of the camera.

Whether your interest is in model photography, art nudes, or even female portraiture, *Model Photography: Techniques and Images in Black & White* is filled with professional tips that will help you create dramatic, softly feminine, and incredibly flattering images of women.

Table of Contents

Interview with Bill Lemon

How long have you been working as a professional photographer?
I first became interested in photography in 1980. I received a lot of support from my friends and my family, and after working part-time out of my apartment for about nine years, I retired from my job and opened my first full-time studio.

What do you see as the advantages of formal training as a photographer? Are there advantages to being self-trained?
When I started out in photography, I took quite a few workshops and they helped me to pick up a lot of little things. As a self-taught photographer, I 've been able to develop a really individual style. A big advantage I can see to formal training is instruction in art and design. I've thought about taking some more formal instruction, but at this point, I'm happy with my style, and so are my clients.

Is most of your model photography commissioned, or is this something you do for personal satisfaction?
None of the photographs in this book were commissioned. They are all images I did with this book in mind, images I shot over the course of several years. Basically, I saw Marco Glaviano's work and thought, "I can do that!" So, I set out to try.

What kind of photography do you do in your studio?
I do all kinds of work! I do table-top, a little portrait, and a few weddings every year (although usually just for friends and former models). The mainstay of my studio is fashion photography. My work has appeared in Studio Photography, Commercial Image, Brides, The Ross Report, and Shutter Bug.

You also teach photography workshops in your area. How did you get started with this?
I started teaching glamour classes in 1992, with a four class series that met once a week in my studio. Afterwards, someone suggested that I think about starting an ongoing workshop, which is what I now do. The "Studio 15 Workshop" meets twice every month, and has about twenty due-paying members. I don't try to teach during these sessions, but rather, we discuss just about every aspect of photography, and do a shoot once every month. My main goal is to keep people motivated and enthusiastic. I love photography and love to share it. That's what this is all about.

How did you become interested in model photography?
I started with model photography! I began by shooting pictures of my girlfriend, and then of her friends. Later, I started photographing co-workers and building up my portfolio. Finally, I showed my work to a local modeling school. They liked it, and I was eventually hired as their primary photographer. I learned a lot from that experience, and especially from the models working there (one of them, Frankie Di, appears in this book).

How has your model photography evolved since you began?
I think it has become a little more artsy, and I know I have learned to work a lot more quickly than I used to. The biggest change has been in my ability to communicate. The more time you spend doing this, the more confident you become about your work and the less intimidated you feel. If you're confident about what you're doing, the model will feel confident, and the image will show it.

What advice would you give to photographers about finding models?

First of all, keep your eyes open everywhere you go, but also be selective. It is very important to get a professional looking business card and carry it with you. If you see someone you would like to photograph, give her your card, and leave it up to her to call you. It's also crucial to put together a portfolio (start by shooting photos of people you know). This shows people that you are legitimate, and helps them get a sense of the quality of your work.

How do you approach working with models?

The most important thing I talk about with any model before her shoot is comfort. If the shoot is strictly fashion, the limit will be set pretty much at lingerie, but with nude or semi-nude, the issue must be addressed up front. I show the model my portfolio. This helps her get a sense of my work. Many find it easier to look at an image and say "I'd be comfortable with something like this," than to explain what they are willing or unwilling to reveal.

Why did you do these images in black and white? Do you do work in color?

All of my fashion work is done in color, but for fine nudes, the contrast and drama of black and white works extremely well. It's almost something you can't put your finger on, but there's a certain mystery to black and white that I just love.

You don't do your own printing. Why did you make this choice?

The biggest factor is that I don't really have the expertise to do it, but additionally, I don't have a darkroom or the space for one in my studio. Time is also an issue. I am fortunate to have a really talented printer, and although its not cheap, I think that with a good printer you can definitely produce outstanding images that reflect your creative vision.

What do you see yourself doing a few years from now? Do you have any new ventures in mind?

I'd love to have the opportunity to do more speaking and to teach more, maybe at some of the workshops that are going on throughout the country. In the end, though, I try to keep things pretty simple: simple equipment, a photographer and a model. I like to do what I do and hope to expand it.

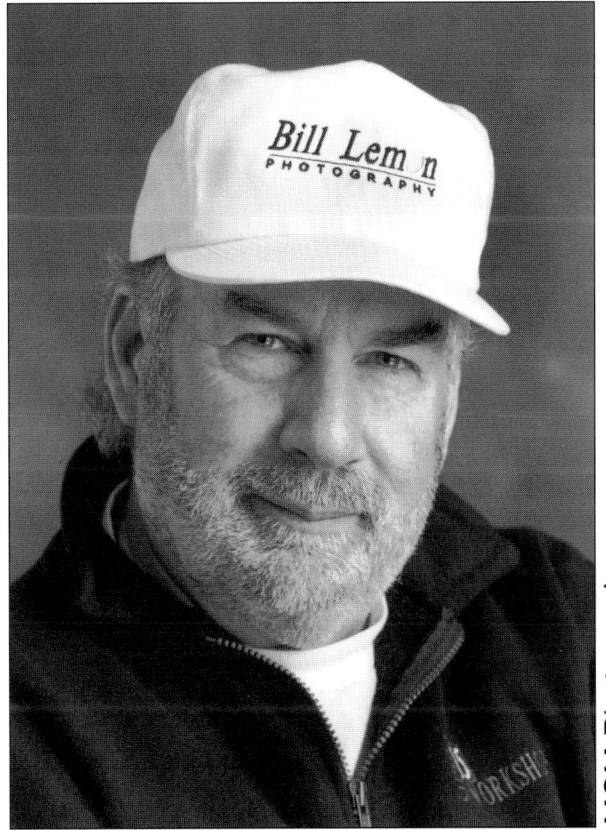

MGM Photography

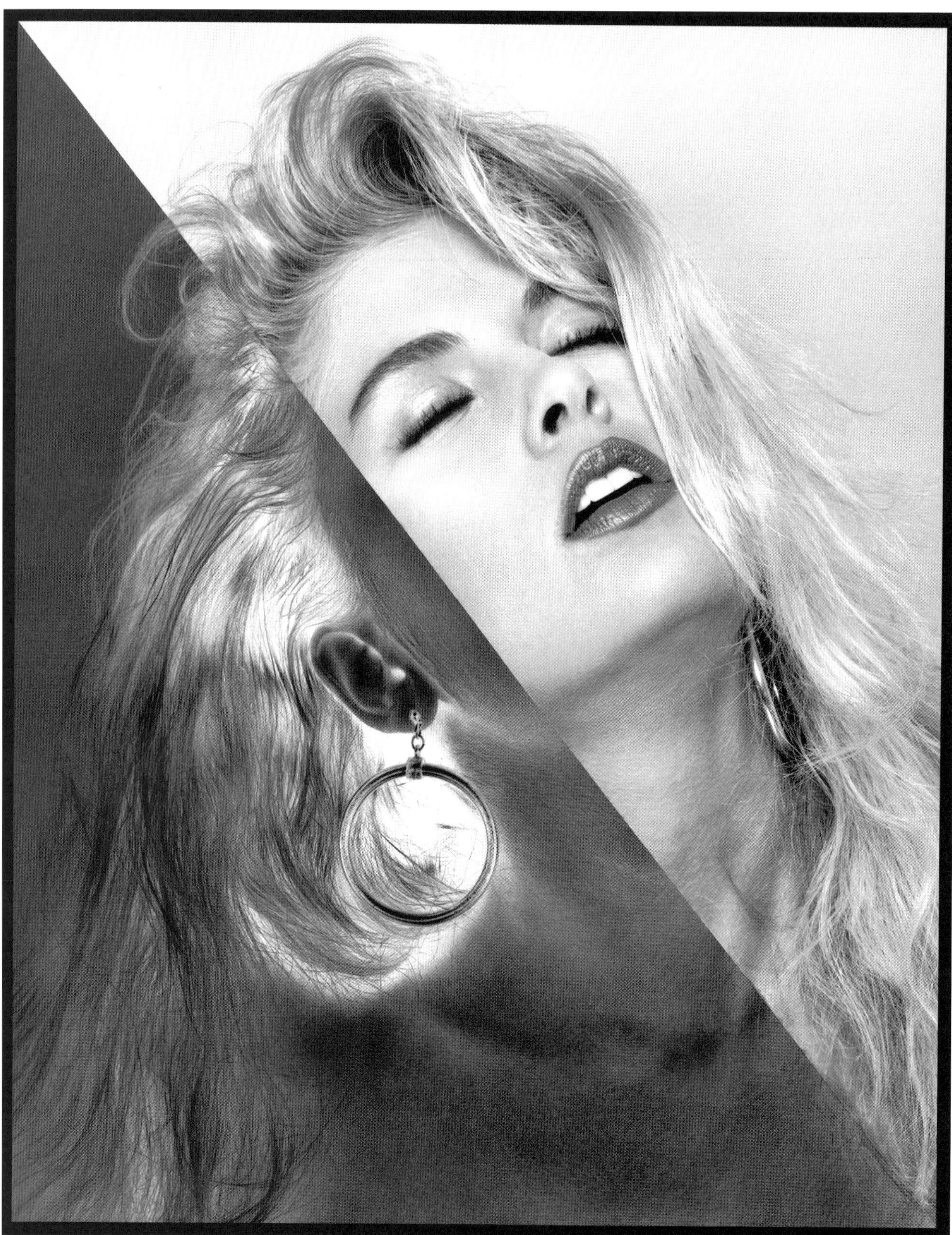

■ Photographer's Comments

This photograph was taken in my studio with two lights. A hair light adds dramatic shine and texture to the model's hair. The main light is positioned directly over the camera. For film, I chose Agfapan 100, which I think gives the best skin tones of all the black & white films on the market today.

■ Posing

The idea for the pose used in this shot came from a picture I saw in a magazine. Fashion magazines are a great resource for ideas when photographing models. With a little experimentation and creativity, basic ideas can be fine-tuned and adapted to create very unique images, such as this one.

■ Printing

Here, it's the unusual printing that makes the image work. A combined effort by the photographer (who conceived of the image) and the printer (who was able to execute it) was required to create this combination positive and negative image. Experiment with printers until you find one who works well with you.

"The setting of the hair light is important and varies with the hair color of the model."

CAMERA
Hasselblad 503

LENS
150mm

FILM
Agfapan 100

LIGHTING
hair light, main light

MODEL
Dale Coleman

■ Natural Light

This classic-looking model with beautiful olive skin was photographed in the early morning light. The morning fog creates a soft background in the space behind her. The model is posed with her back to the East, but her face is turned toward the sun which had just begun to rise in the morning sky.

While fancy lighting set-ups can certainly provide great results, it would be a mistake to overlook the beautiful images that can be created with natural lighting alone. Remember, too, that a lot of lights can be intimidating, especially to people who are not used to being professionally photographed. Using available light can often make your model feel more at ease. In this photo, the morning sun does a wonderful job of illuminating the model's face, chest and legs, and emphasizes the beautiful lines of her body in this pose.

■ Clothing

The dramatic print of the robe (which the model provided) is also an important component of this image. The circular print of the flowers contrasts elegantly with the sharp linearity of the grasses and twigs all around the model.

■ Printing

The edges of the image were darkened and a white border added. Embellishments like these can make an image truly unique.

BILL LEMON'S HINTS AND TIPS:

Different models will have different levels of comfort when it comes to nude or semi-nude shots. This model was not comfortable with a nude image. However, by dressing her in a low-cut bra and allowing her robe to fall open, a very sensual image is created without any nudity at all. It is important to discuss with your models the kind of image they feel comfortable creating.

CAMERA
Hasselblad 503

LENS
150mm

FILM
Agfapan 100

LIGHTING
early morning natural light

MODEL
Annie Wanberg

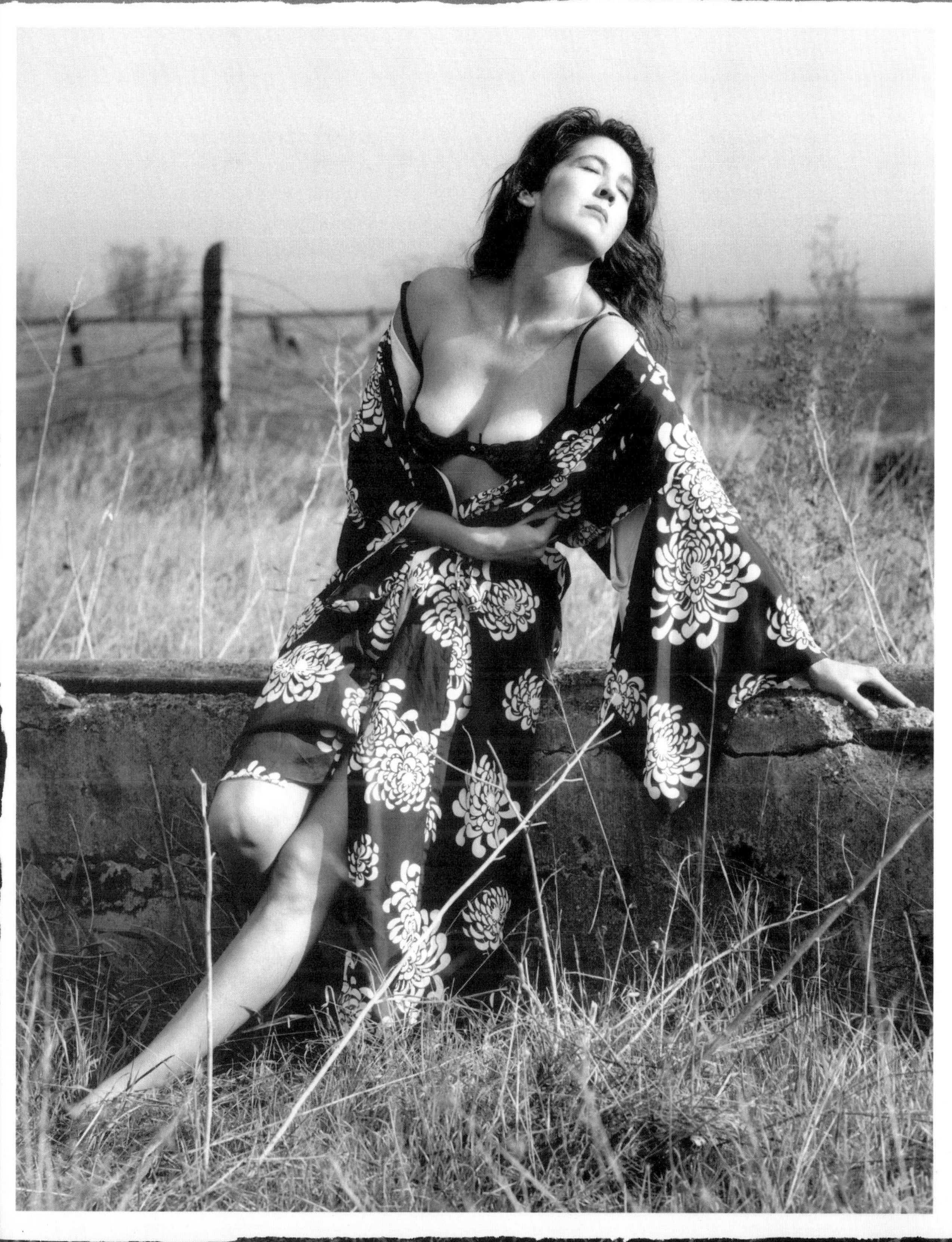

■ Lighting

This studio portrait relies on a two light system. There is a main light positioned over the camera, and a hair light. The setting of the hair light is important and varies with the hair color of the model. For dark hair, a two stop difference between the hair light and the main light usually produces good results. For light hair, reduce the difference to one stop. Of course this is only a general rule of thumb, but I find that it works well for the majority of images.

■ Reflector

The addition of a silver reflector to the lighting system is crucial to the creation of this image. For this photo, a reflector was placed in front of the model on a drafting table. It was inclined slightly toward her face. This reflector is what causes the catch-lights on the lower part of her eyes and fills in the nose, chin and lip shadows.

■ Sharper Images

The use of a medium format camera has a lot to do with the amount of texture detail (on the lips, for instance), but whether you shoot with a medium format or 35mm camera, I strongly recommend the use of a tripod and cable release. This is a key factor in eliminating any camera movement, and creating images with extremely sharp detail.

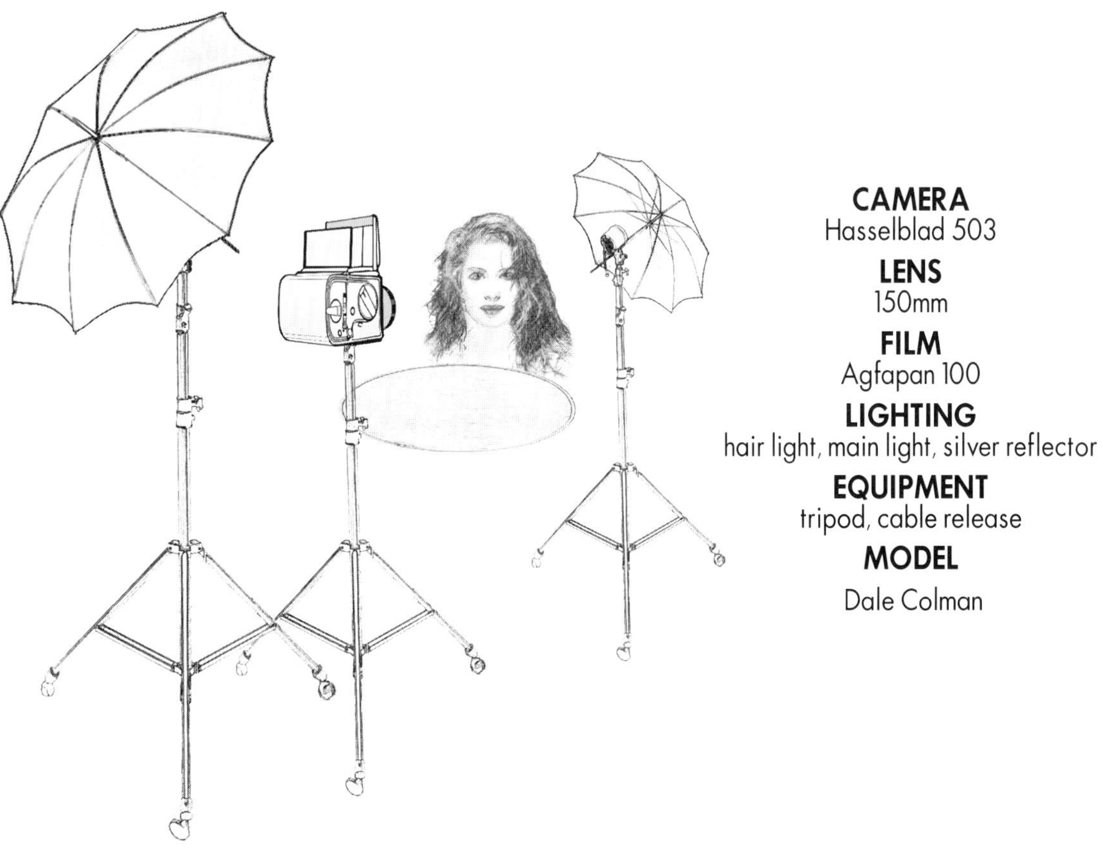

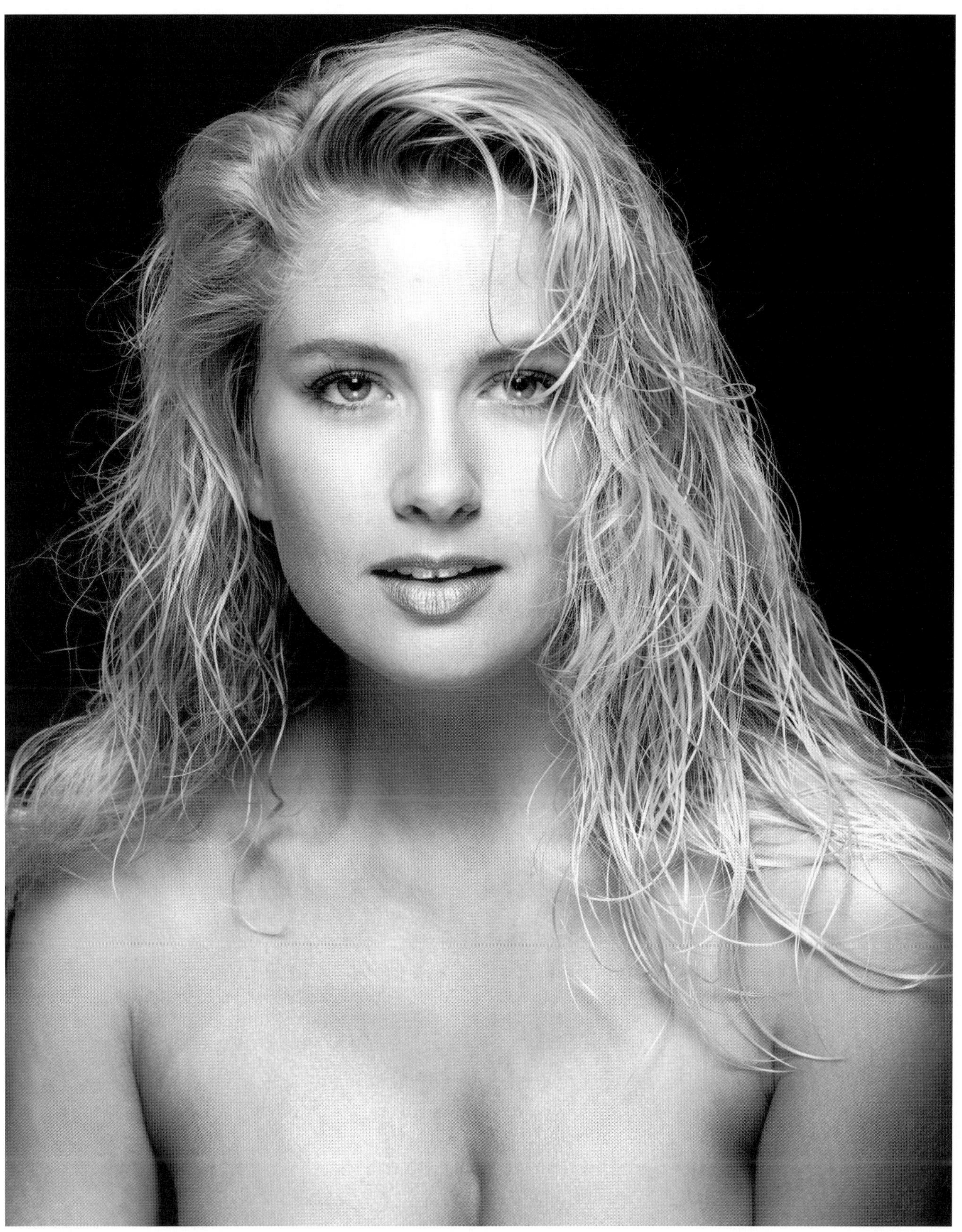

■ Setting

The barn in which this image was shot is a favorite spot of mine, and you will see it used again and again throughout this book. It's a site which I discovered by chance, but since securing permission from the owner, I have shot here repeatedly.

Although it may not initially look like a place you'd imagine taking sensual pictures of beautiful women, the contrast between the rugged character of the setting and the soft beauty of the women is extremely effective. Using uncommon and unexpected settings can often add an interesting dimension to an image. Do make sure, though, when shooting on location, to obtain permission from the owner of the property.

■ Natural Light

Here, the late afternoon sun is the sole source of light and contributes to the deep shadows which emphasize the curves of the model's body. The model was positioned outside at the southern wall of the barn. Light from the west emphasizes the texture of her damp skin, the boards of the barn, and her clothing.

■ Composition

The model's medium length hair is pulled to the side to reveal her neck and lengthen the line of her body.

■ Printing

Printing this 8"x10" image on 11"x14" paper gives it the impression of being matted.

BILL LEMON'S HINTS AND TIPS:

When shooting on location, try to look at your setting with a creative eye. Even if you have previously decided on a series of poses, a good setting will often inspire you to envision new poses. Pay special attention to natural light phenomena (such as light beams through the boards of an old barn). These can often be used to your advantage.

CAMERA
Hasselblad 503

LENS
150mm

FILM
Kodak TMX 100

LIGHTING
natural late afternoon sun

MODEL
Jennifer Tovani

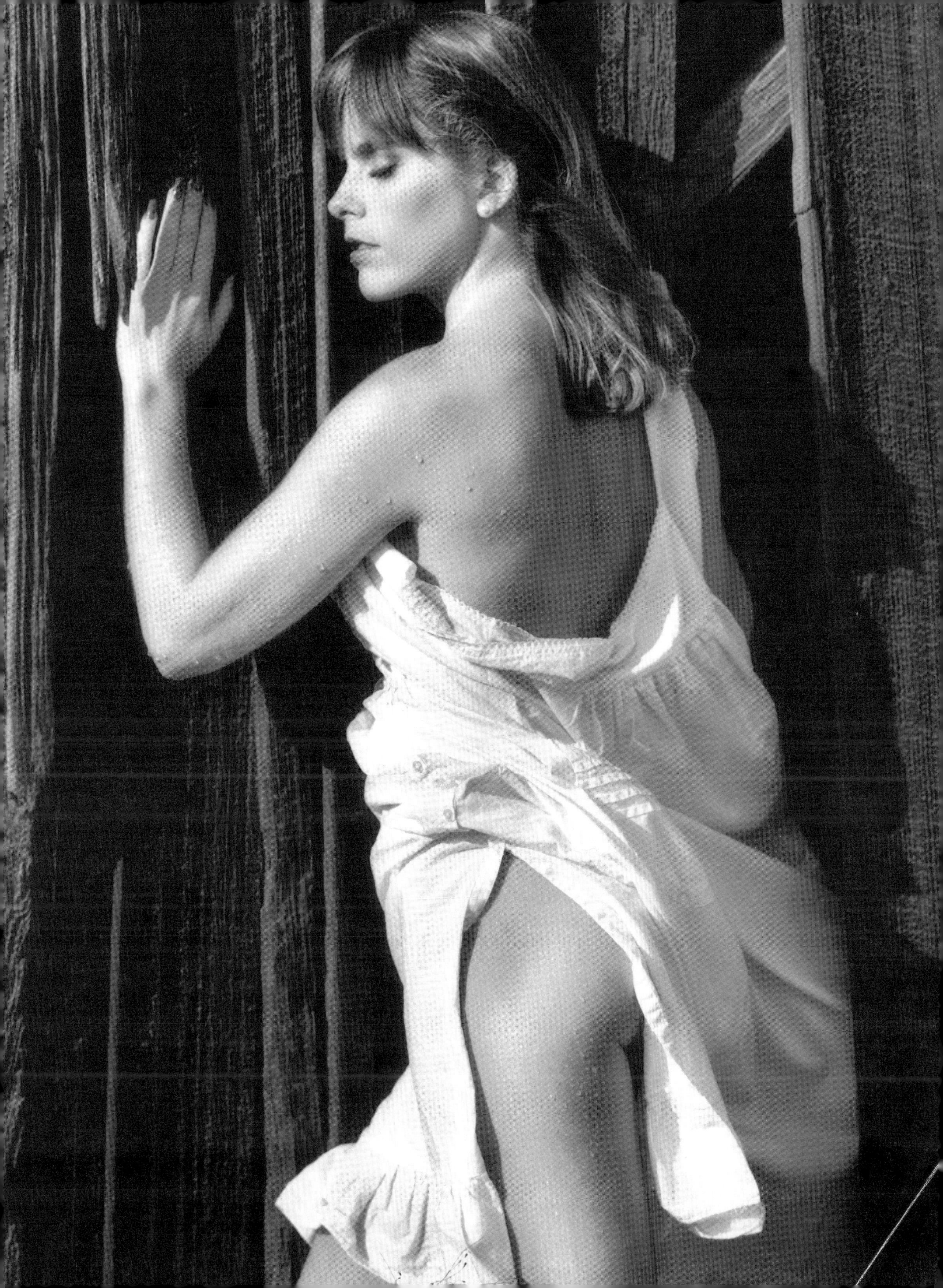

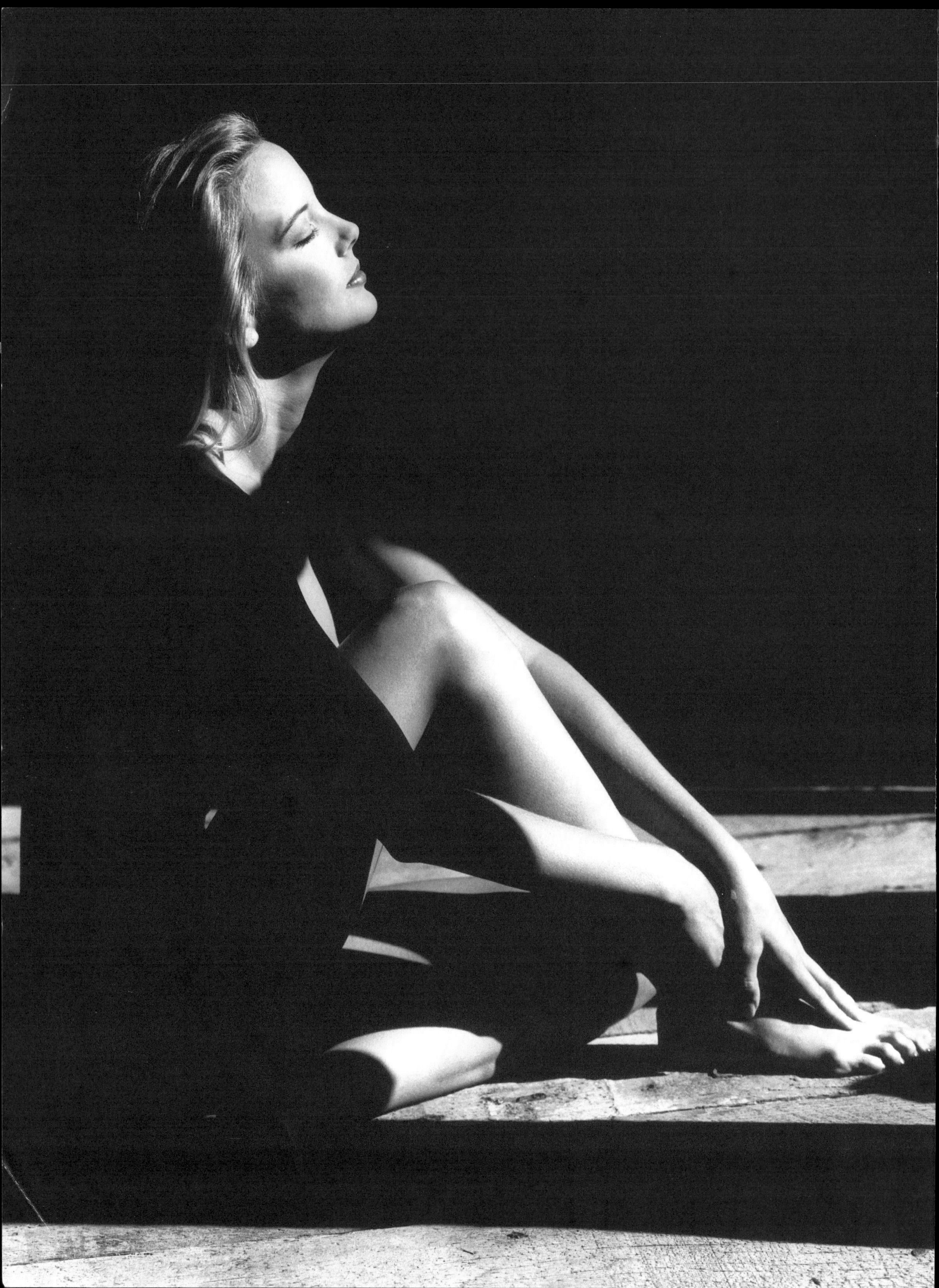

■ Finding a Model

The vast majority of the models I work with have at least some professional modeling experience. Still, it never hurts to be on the lookout for subjects who might work for an image you have in mind, or whose unique beauty suggests new images. For instance, I met this model while taking pictures at a Christmas party. It's usually a good idea to simply propose a sitting and leave your business card with potential models. Leave it to them to call you if they are interested.

■ Setting

This photo was shot inside an old barn. All of the light comes from the early morning sun streaming through gaps between the barn boards.

■ Posing

The model was nude for this shot, but her body is almost completely shrouded in dark shadow. This technique is good for creating nudes of subjects who are timid about revealing too much to the camera.

■ Composition

Despite the fact that we see relatively little of the model, this image is made captivating by its composition. Notice how the light draws your eye diagonally down the page. The backward tilt of the model's head (aligning her facial profile with the angle of her lower leg) helps to create this attractive line. The smooth curve of her hair, the glow of her skin, and the delicate crossing of her hands serve to soften the image, making it sensual and feminine.

BILL LEMON'S HINTS AND TIPS:
The more comfortable your model feels, and the more she feels able to trust you, the better chance you have of capturing pleasing images of her. Being in front of the camera makes many people nervous. It's important to talk with your model and discuss her comfort level with various clothes and poses.

CAMERA
Pentax 6x7
LENS
200mm
FILM
Kodak Plus X 100
LIGHTING
early morning light
MODEL
Michelle Piper

■ Lighting

This model was photographed at the doorway in front of an old barn. The natural light hits her from the right so that her body disappears into the shadows behind the door. About thirty feet behind her, a large and bright section of broken out boards is allowed to go softly out of focus by shooting at 5.6*f*.

■ Camera Tilt

Gently tilting the camera adds an interesting perspective to this shot. It's a technique I use frequently, and one I recommend to students as an easy way of adding another dimension to their images. It's an easy way to breathe new life into an otherwise familiar pose.

I would suggest two guidelines for those wishing to try this technique. First, don't go too far. A small tilt will add emphasis to a pose. Notice how the tilt in this photo calls attention to the model's hip. If you turn the picture so that the model is perfectly vertical, you notice that this curve seems to become less pronounced. Too great a tilt will make the model look off balance. Aim for something that looks natural. It's not hard to imagine that this model was simply leaning on a door that just happened to be tilted.

HINTS AND TIPS

If a particular style or piece of clothing is integral to an image you have in mind, be prepared to go out and buy it. I purchased the garments featured in this photo after seeing a similar camisole in a magazine layout. Its ultra-feminine look in contrast with the rugged look of the barn is part of what makes this image work.

CAMERA
Hasselblad 503
LENS
150mm
FILM
Kodak TMX 100
LIGHTING
natural
EQUIPMENT
tripod and cable release
MODEL
Carrie Zanolini

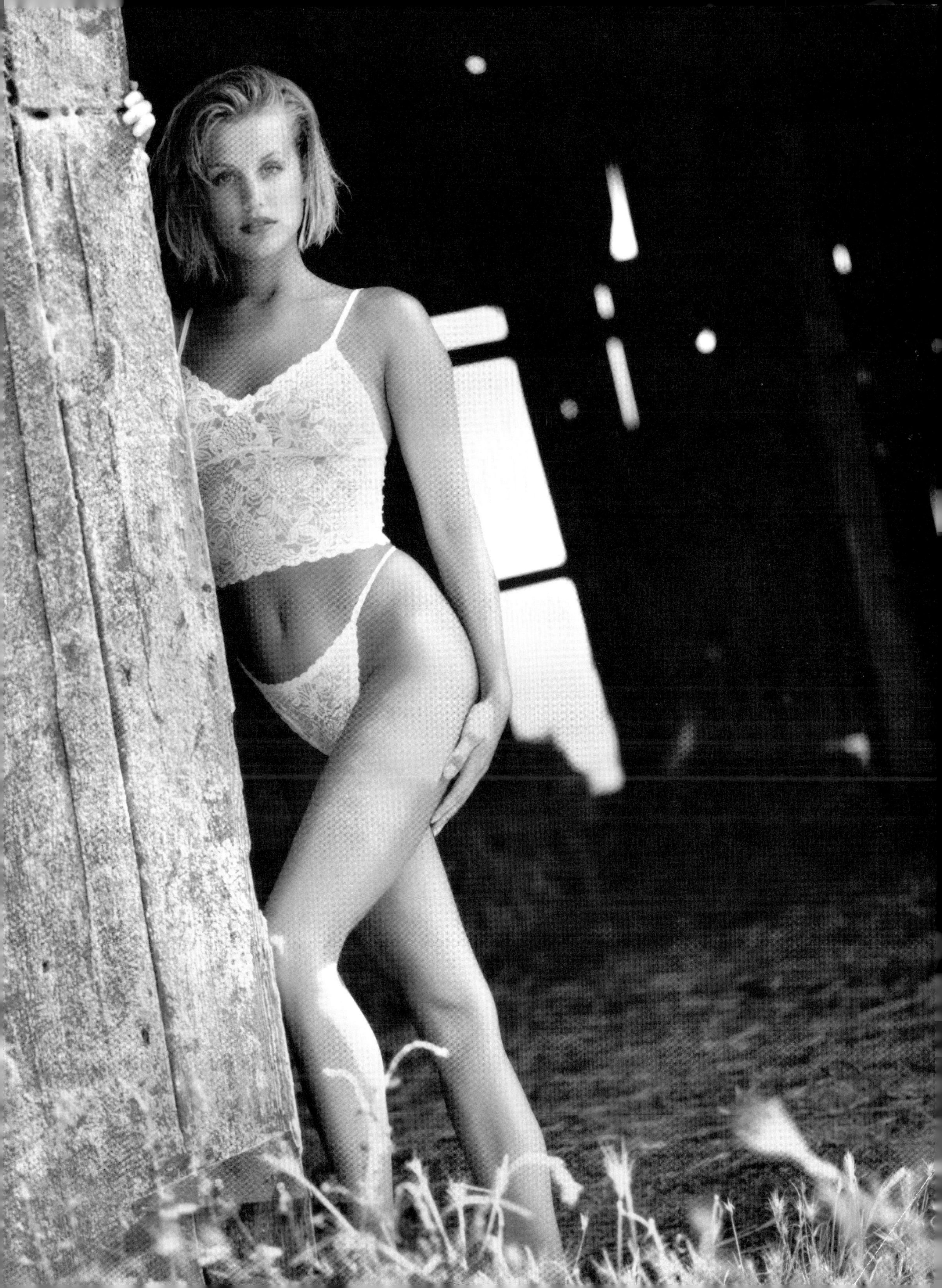

■ **Model Selection**
This is a good example of a shot that I conceived of long before I found a model to work with on it. The picture was taken in front of the make-up mirror in my studio, and required the model to sit on the counter. Because the counter is small, I needed to find a model who was not too tall to pose there comfortably.

■ **Lighting**
A large softbox was positioned far to the right of the model so as to eliminate glare in the mirror.

■ **Shooting**
The camera is focussed not on the model (who is allowed to go into soft focus), but on her reflection in the mirror.

■ **Clothing**
I shot this image with the model both fully nude and with the unbuttoned vest (seen here). In the end, the partially clothed version (although it is just as revealing) seemed a better choice. One factor is the way that that white vest works with the white walls and door reflected in the mirror, and creates another area of contrast. The open garment is also very sensual, and fits the tone of the image.

"I shot this image with the model both fully nude and with the unbuttoned vest..."

CAMERA
Hasselblad 503
LENS
150 mm
FILM
Agfapan 100
LIGHTING
large soft box
MODEL
Kirsten Harrison

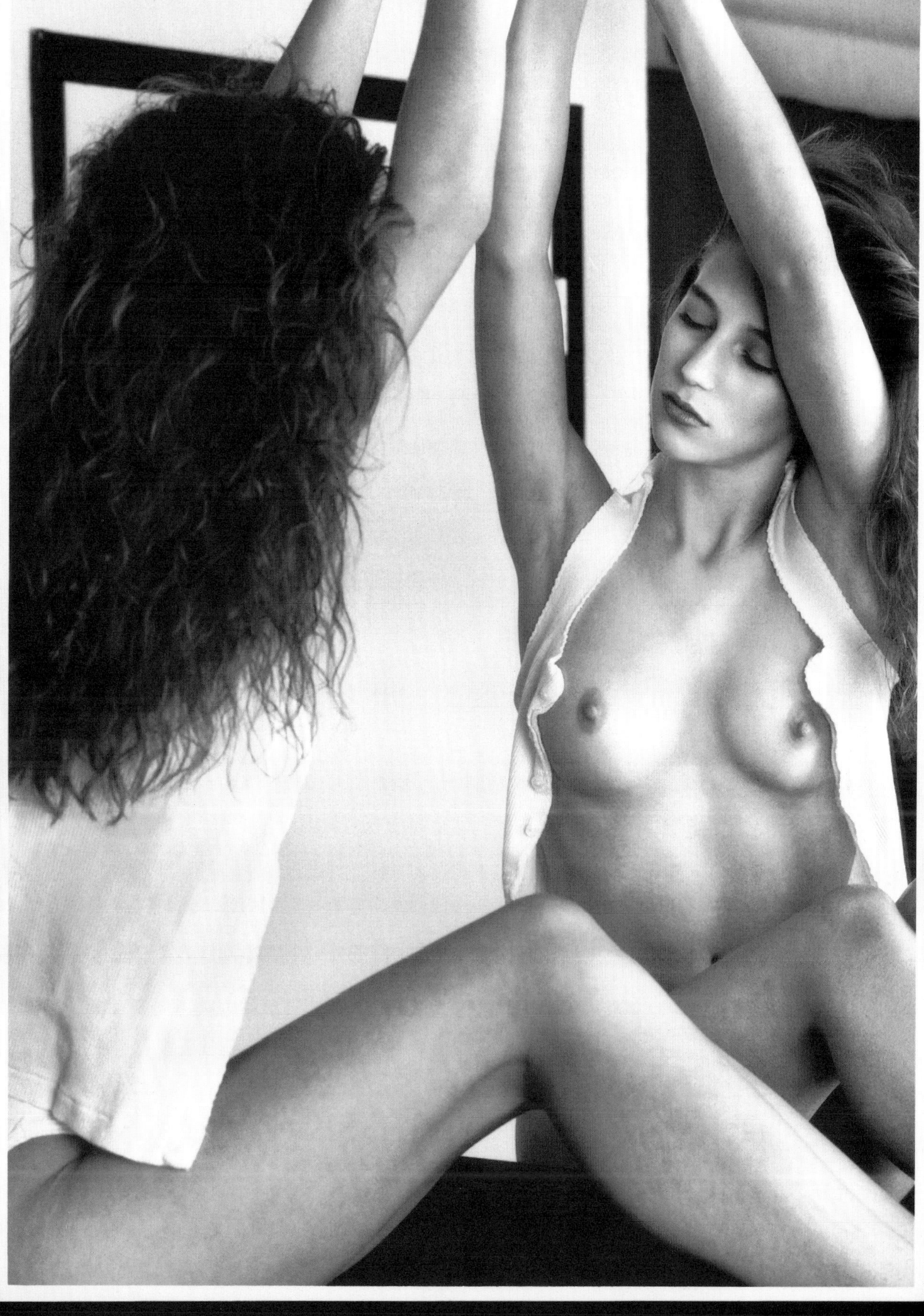

■ Posing and Composition

This image is of a somewhat different flavor than most of those found in this volume. The model's eyes and lips are extremely vivid, a factor emphasized by the full frontal aspect of the shot. Her pose (arms crossed) is also a powerful one. Rather than leaving the model's hair long and loose, here it is pulled back for a more sleek look. While the image is highly sensual, it is not so much playful as mature, refined and intense.

■ Printing

Here the sharp white border makes the image seem to pop off of the paper.

■ Lighting and Reflector

This studio portrait relies on a two light system. There is a main light positioned over the camera, and a hair light. For this photo, a reflector was also placed in front of the model on a drafting table. It was inclined slightly toward her face. This reflector is what causes the catch-lights on the lower part of her eyes and fills in the nose, chin and lip shadows.

CAMERA
Hasselblad 503

LENS
150mm

FILM
Agfapan 100

LIGHTING
main light, hair light, silver reflector

MODEL
Dale Colman

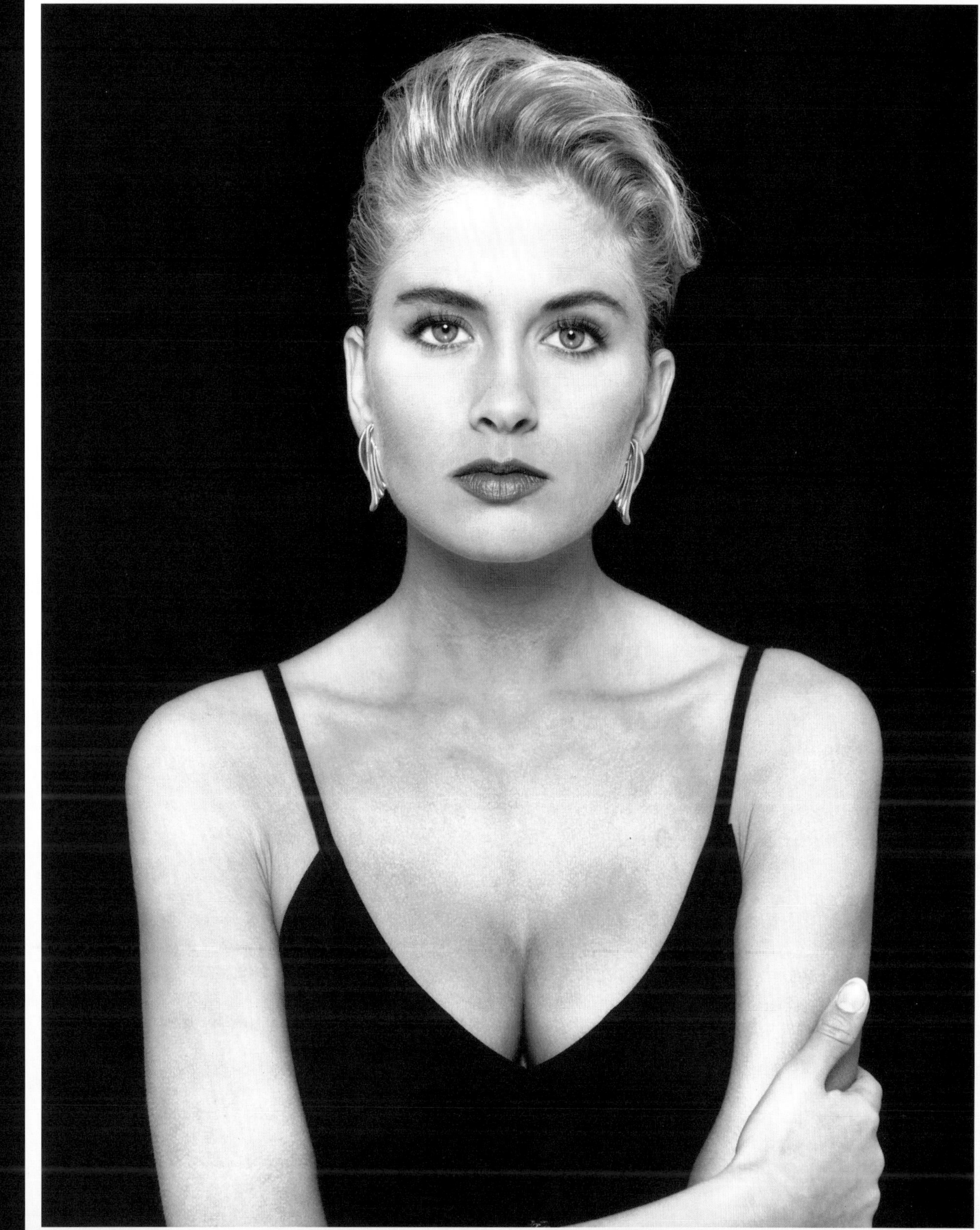

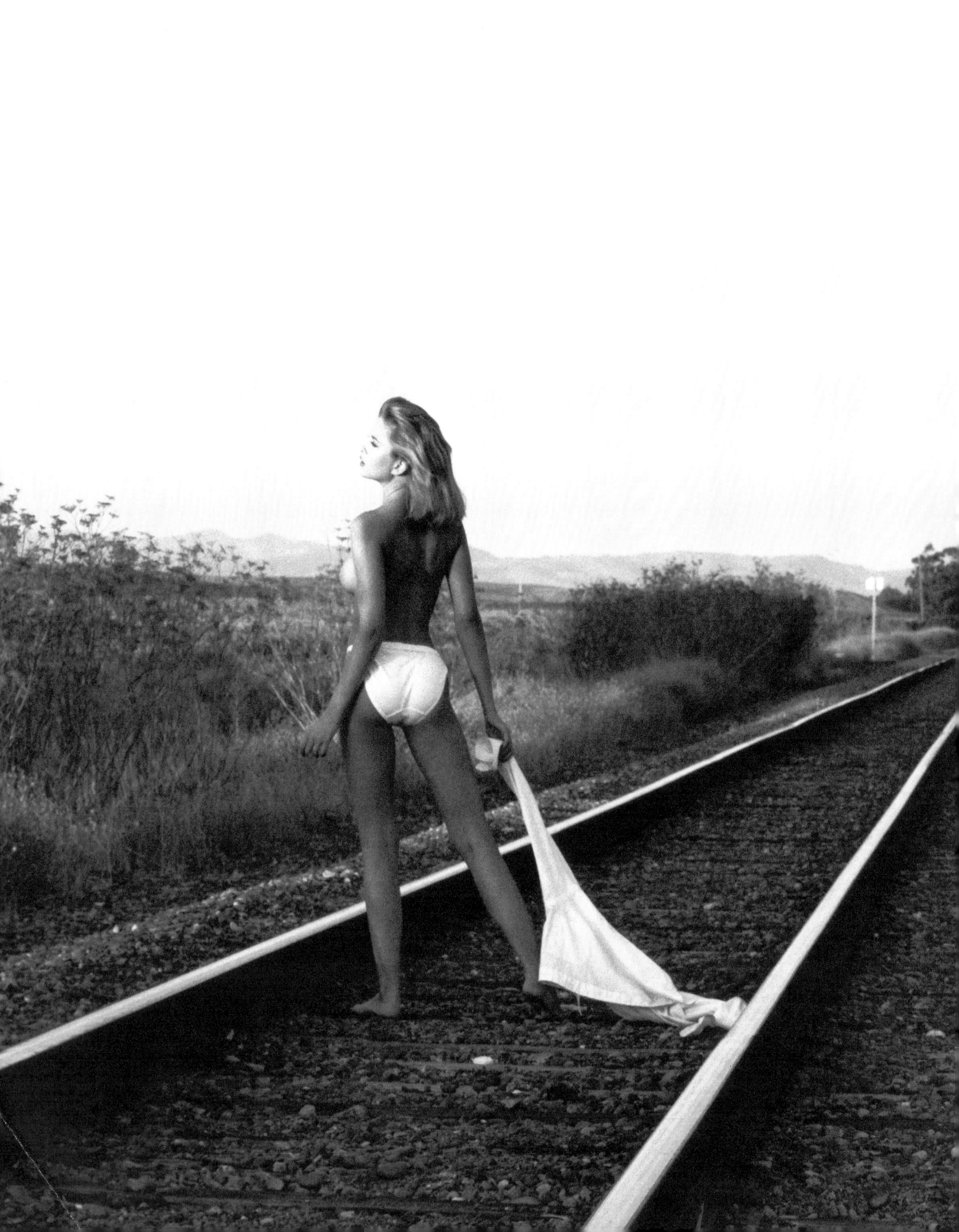

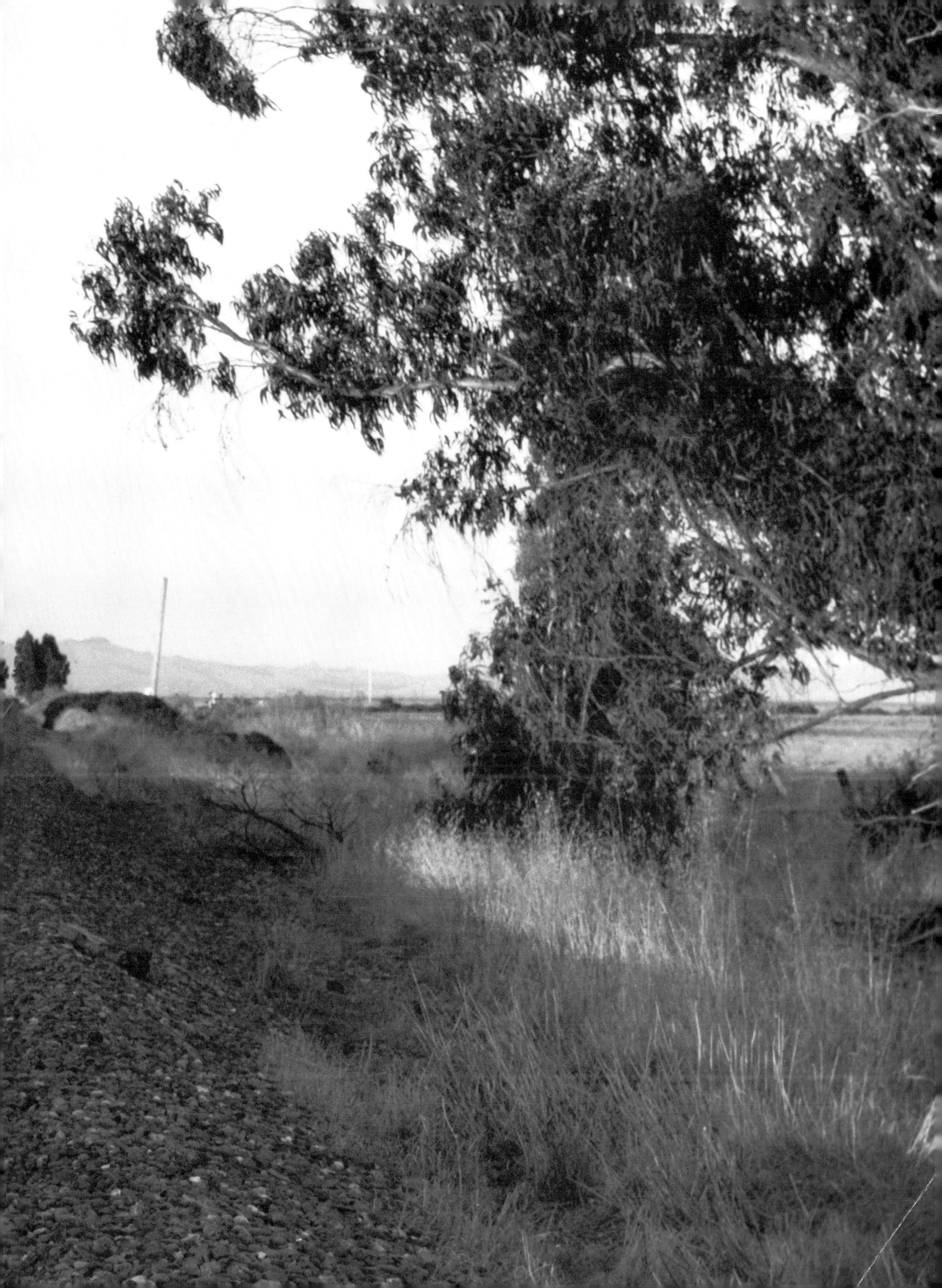

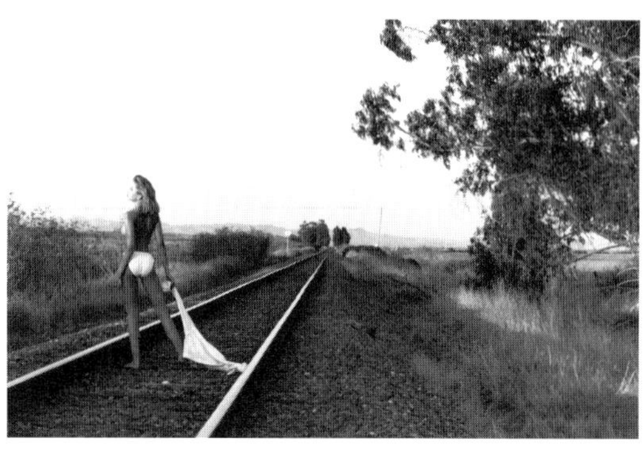

■ Film
I selected a 400 speed film for this shot in order to achieve an extreme depth of field.

■ Posing
The model's face is turned toward the sun. Her right heel is slightly lifted, causing a shift in her hips. Her body is turned so that the sun just catches the side of her breast.

■ Composition
The shirt which trails the ground beside the model, plays an important role in the composition. The huge expanse of bright sky takes up a large part of the image; the model is situated in a darker corner of the photograph, but the high contrast spot of brightness created by the shirt draws the viewer's attention to her. Sufficient light shows on the train tracks which create so much of the sense of vastness in the image.

■ Texture
Here there are interesting textural variations between the soft skin, the metal train tracks, the stones of the railway bed, the trees and grasses, and the mountains in the distance. Simple settings with intriguing textures can be very visually appealing.

BILL LEMON'S HINTS AND TIPS:
Take your images one step further by adding a narrative element, such as this picture suggests. Often a story can be created simply by the choice of setting, Here we are left to wonder why this woman is on the train tracks. Has she said farewell to a lover? Is she waiting for someone to return? Is she remembering the love she had to leave behind?

CAMERA
Hasselblad 503

LENS
80mm

FILM
Ilford 400 XP2

LIGHTING
late afternoon sun

MODEL
Dale Colman

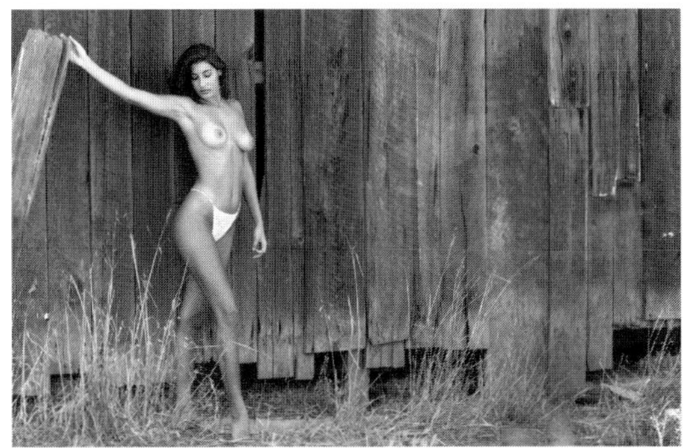

■ Foreground

Don't be afraid to leave grasses in the foreground (or to leave anything in the image which can be made to work to your advantage). It may be tempting to knock something like this out of the way, but remember that these elements can very often add an interesting texture or layer of visual information to your image.

■ Composition

If ten photographers were given the chance to shoot this same model in the same pose and setting, many would not add the second page of the image. But the second page is important because it allows us to see more as if we were looking upon this scene in real life. The human scope of vision is not limited to a 8"x10" field. By creating a wider view, a new dimension is added to the photograph.

■ Clothing

The high French cut of her underwear is integral to the image, since it has the visual effect of lengthening her legs. This high cut is usually most flattering.

BILL LEMON'S HINTS AND TIPS:
Purchase the best tripod you can afford. This is not a place to skimp, since it is an integral component in achieving clear, clean images. When shopping for a cable release, it is not always necessary to go with the priciest one. I have found that Nikon, for instance, makes relatively inexpensive releases that work extremely well.

CAMERA
Hasselblad 503
LENS
150mm
FILM
Agfapan 100
LIGHTING
natural
EQUIPMENT
tripod and cable release
MODEL
Lalanya Hudspeth

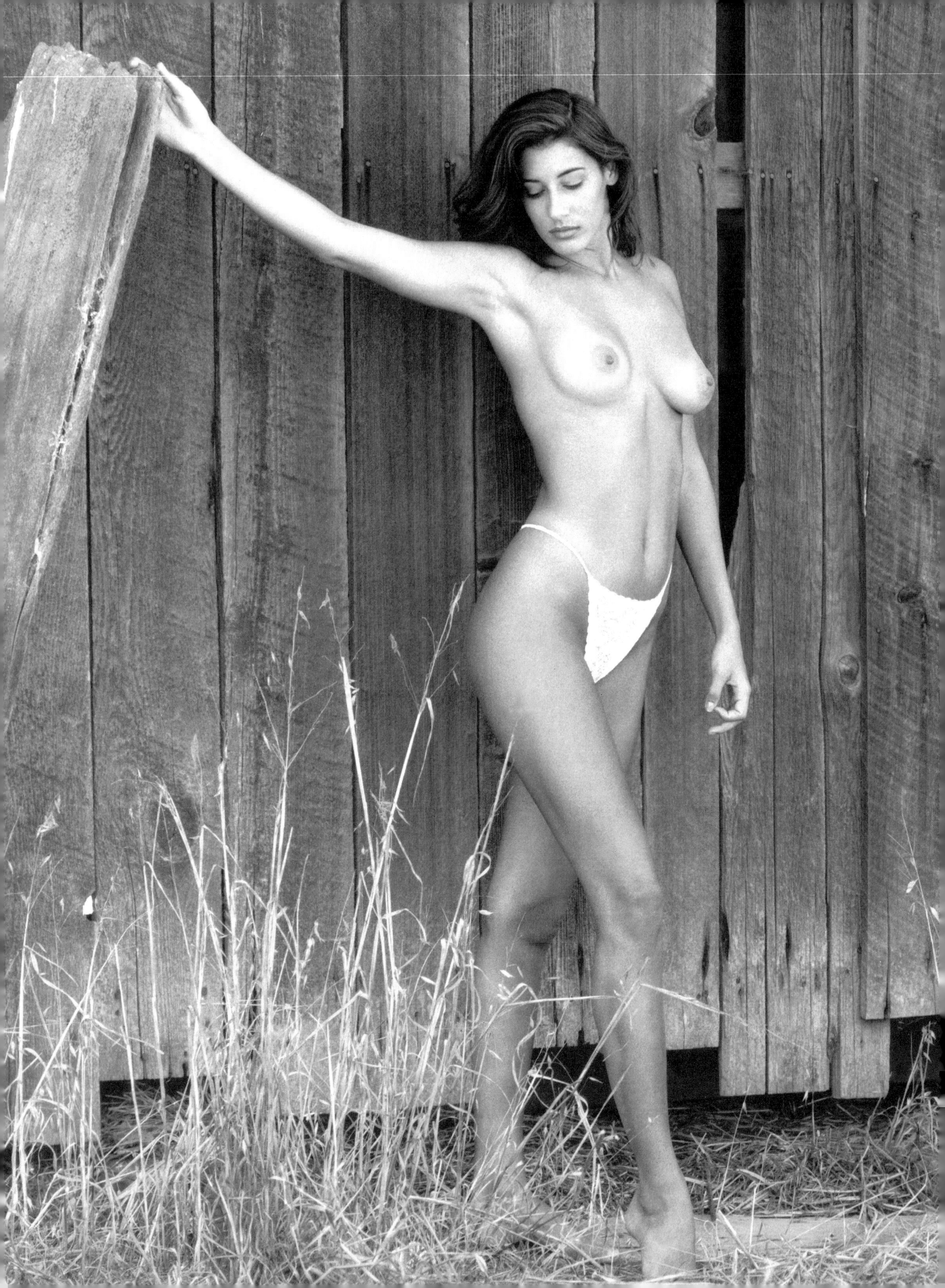

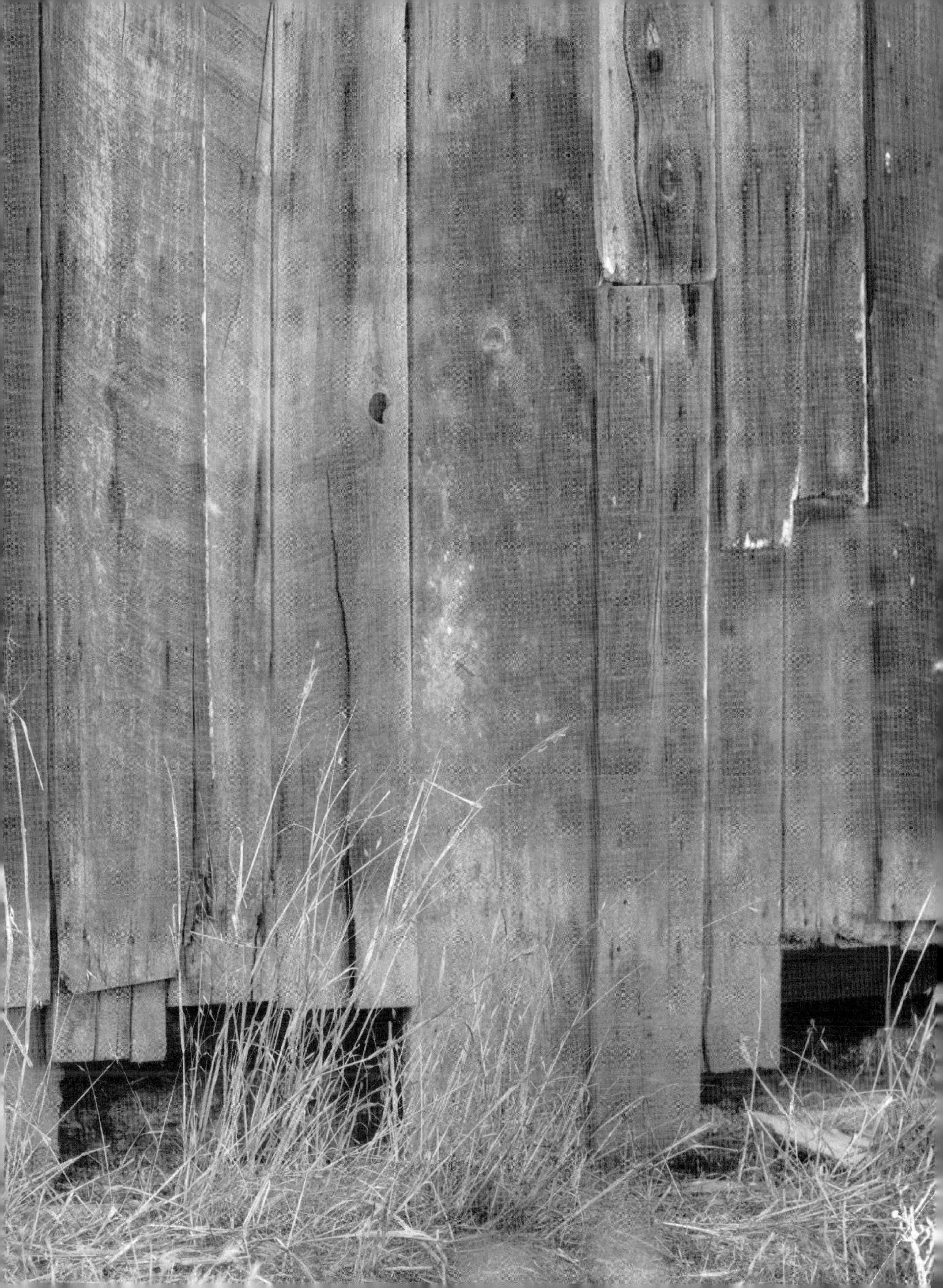

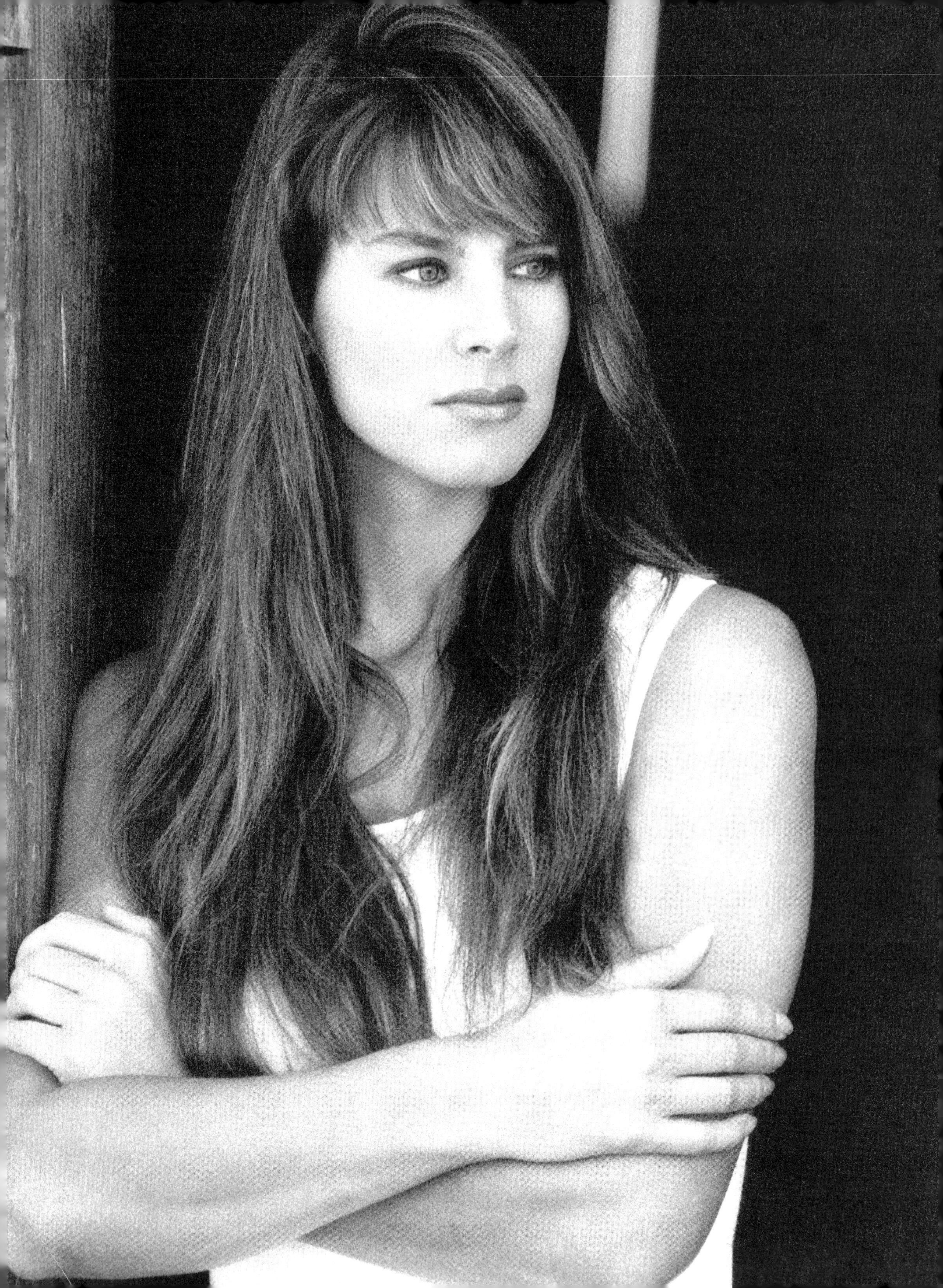

■ Film

Because I was looking for a soft grain in this image, I selected Kodak TMZ 3200, but rated it at 1600. Since this film is only available in a 35mm format, the choice of film also dictated my choice of camera.

■ Posing

The three-quarter view on this model is a strong and sensual pose, but not a playful as some of the others in this book. The northern light on the model's face and body is perfect for this type of image.

■ Cropping

Note that the model is not centered in the frame. Rather, as she looks off to her left, the space there enhances and extends her gaze. This gives the photo an added dimension that is achieved by creative cropping. Centering an image is not always the answer to questions of composition.

"The three-quarter view on this model is a strong and sensual pose."

CAMERA
Nikon F3
LENS
180mm
FILM
Kodak TMZ 3200 rated at 1600
LIGHTING
natural
MODEL
Annette McKnight

■ The Model

Looks can often be deceiving, and a good model may be capable of many different looks. Although the model here appears every inch the image of solitude and peace, her personality really tends toward the vivacious and lively. Be prepared to work with a model's many possibilities!

■ Lighting

Here, the model faces East as the sunlight hits her from the Southeast. The grass in the foreground also catches this southerly light and adds depth to the image.

■ Clothing

The model here is very sensual, but that the photo is not very revealing. This is achieved by using clothing strategically. Here, a shirt pulled around her shoulders and draping over her thighs covers her body, but suggests sensuality.

■ Setting

I chose this particularly quiet setting because I wanted to capture a sense of solitude and peace.

"...a good model may be capable of many different looks."

CAMERA
Hasselblad 503

LENS
150 mm

FILM
Kodak TMX 100

LIGHTING
natural, midafternoon

EQUIPMENT
tripod

MODEL
Stephanie Perivaloris

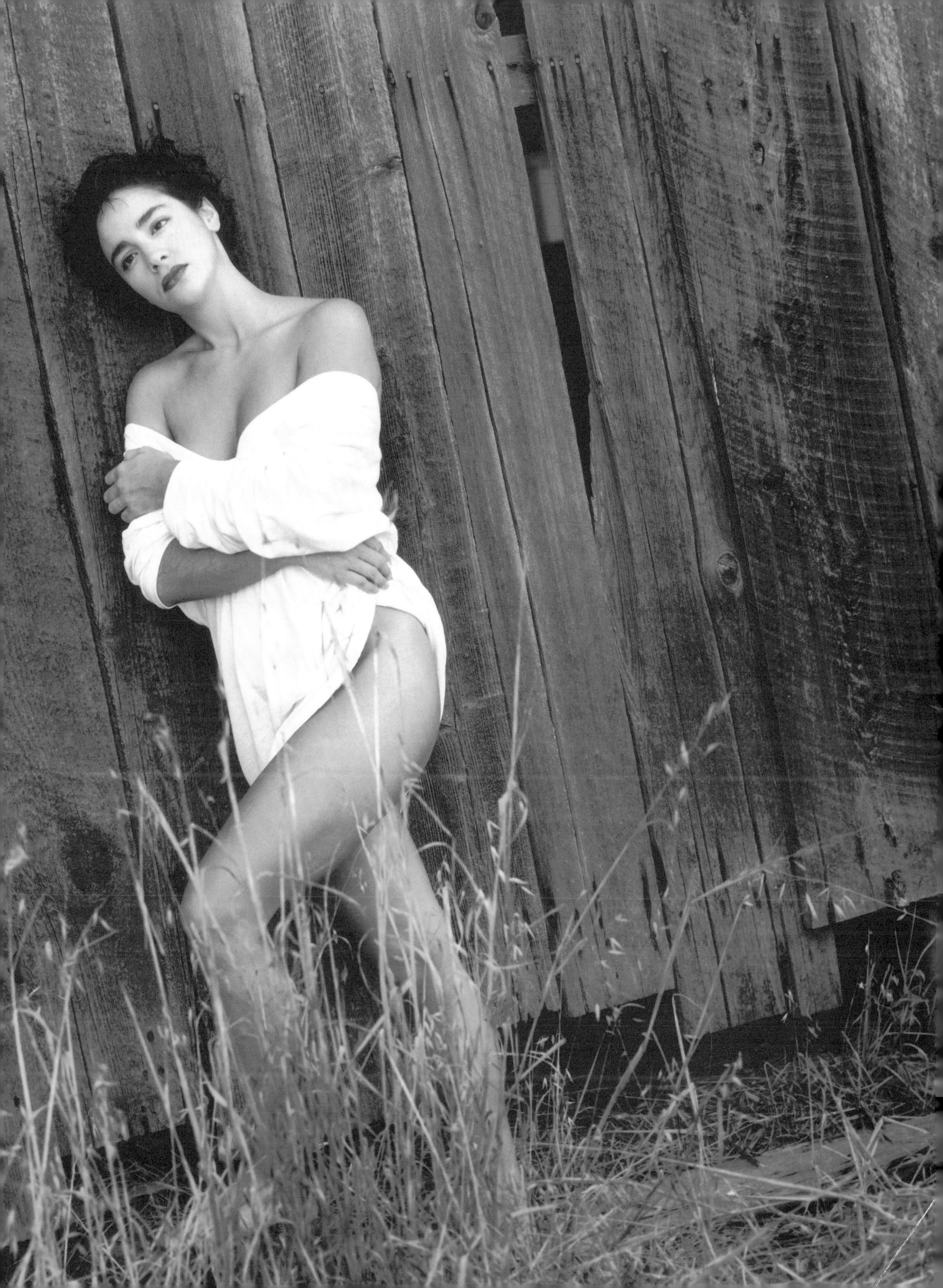

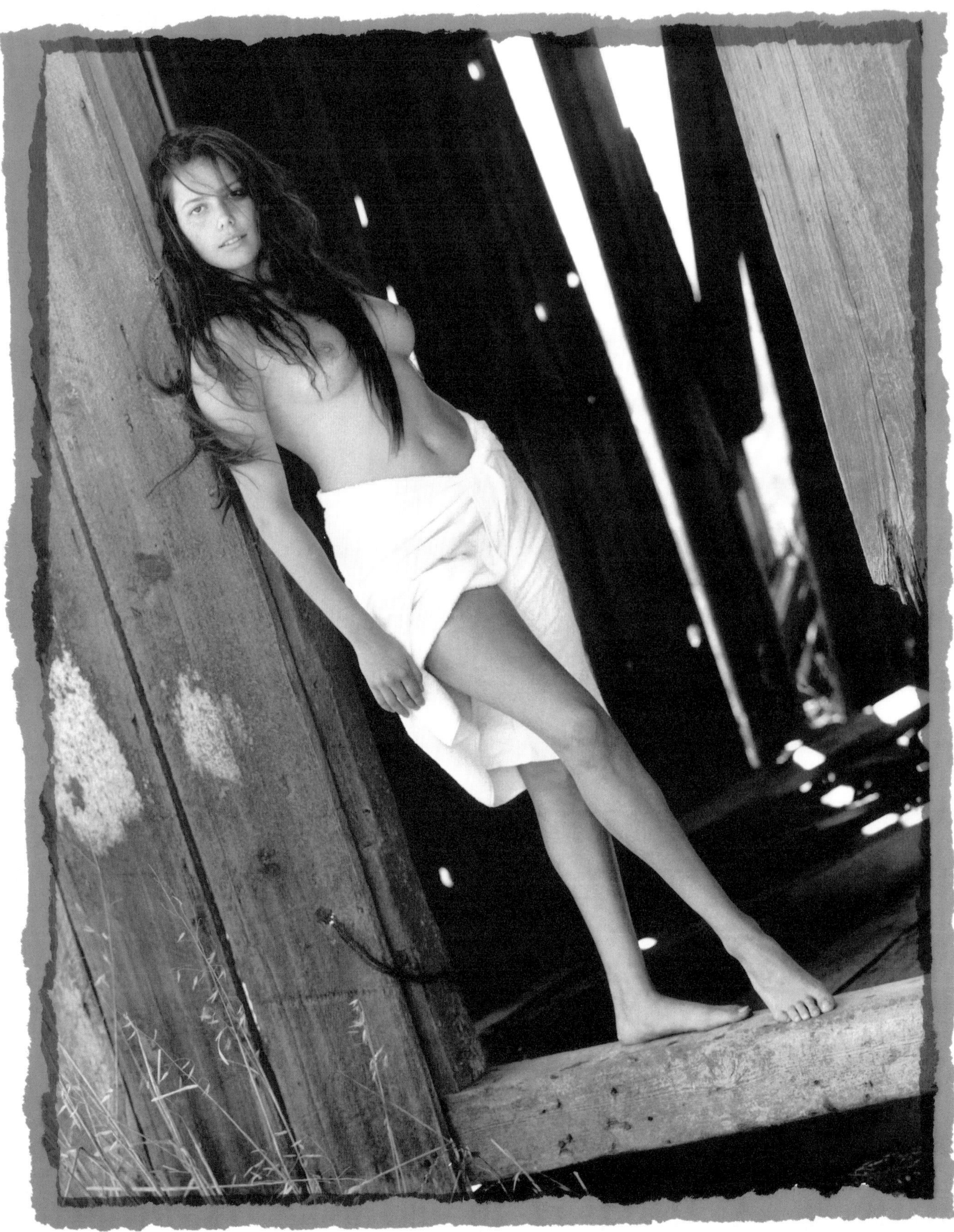

■ Model Selection

I had wanted to shoot this image for a long time before I found the right model for it. Be on the lookout for great images and settings, even if you don't have the right model quite yet. You may have to experiment with several models before you find one with the perfect look.

■ Camera

Here again, the selection of a medium format camera makes a world of difference in rendering the textures found in this image (examine the towel, the wood and the grasses). The tilt of the camera also contributes an added dimension.

■ Printing

Creating an image doesn't end with the click of the shutter. In this image, for example, a rustic-looking border gives the photograph an extra area of interest.

This border was created using a system of four overlays (which can be constructed out of cardboard or gel material). This kind of special printing is never cheap, but when negotiating a price, you may want to remind the printer that (once it is set up) this kind of printing can be repeated for other customers.

BILL LEMON'S HINTS AND TIPS:

Don't settle for simply taking a picture of a beautiful woman. Find a way to incorporate her in a setting; the foreground and background are an important part of the image as a whole. Here, the texture and composition of grass in the foreground and the barn boards in the background are integral to the flavor of the photograph.

CAMERA
Hasselblad 503
LENS
150mm
FILM
Kodak TMX 100
LIGHTING
natural
MODEL
Alysha Haran

■ Setting

The incredible texture of the chipped paint on this old crane made it an ideal location to shoot a very interesting image. The farm equipment is nicely complemented by the equally rustic border of the print.

■ Clothing

To create images like this, it is important to choose clothes which will add to the character of the image. Clothes can effectively highlight features of the body (or enticingly concealing them), as well as add texture and points of emphasis.

The model posed in white, since darker colored garments would have made her image disappear into the shadows in which she is posed.

When shooting black and white images, keep in mind that very dark or very light clothes will produce the most dramatic results. For example, this image would have less impact if her garments were in a mid-tone grey. If shooting in direct sunlight, bear in mind that white clothes tend to get overexposed, and will usually have to be burned down during printing.

"...very dark or very light clothes will produce the most dramatic results."

CAMERA
Hasselblad 503
LENS
150 mm
FILM
Agfapan 100
LIGHTING
natural
MODEL
Carrie Zanolini

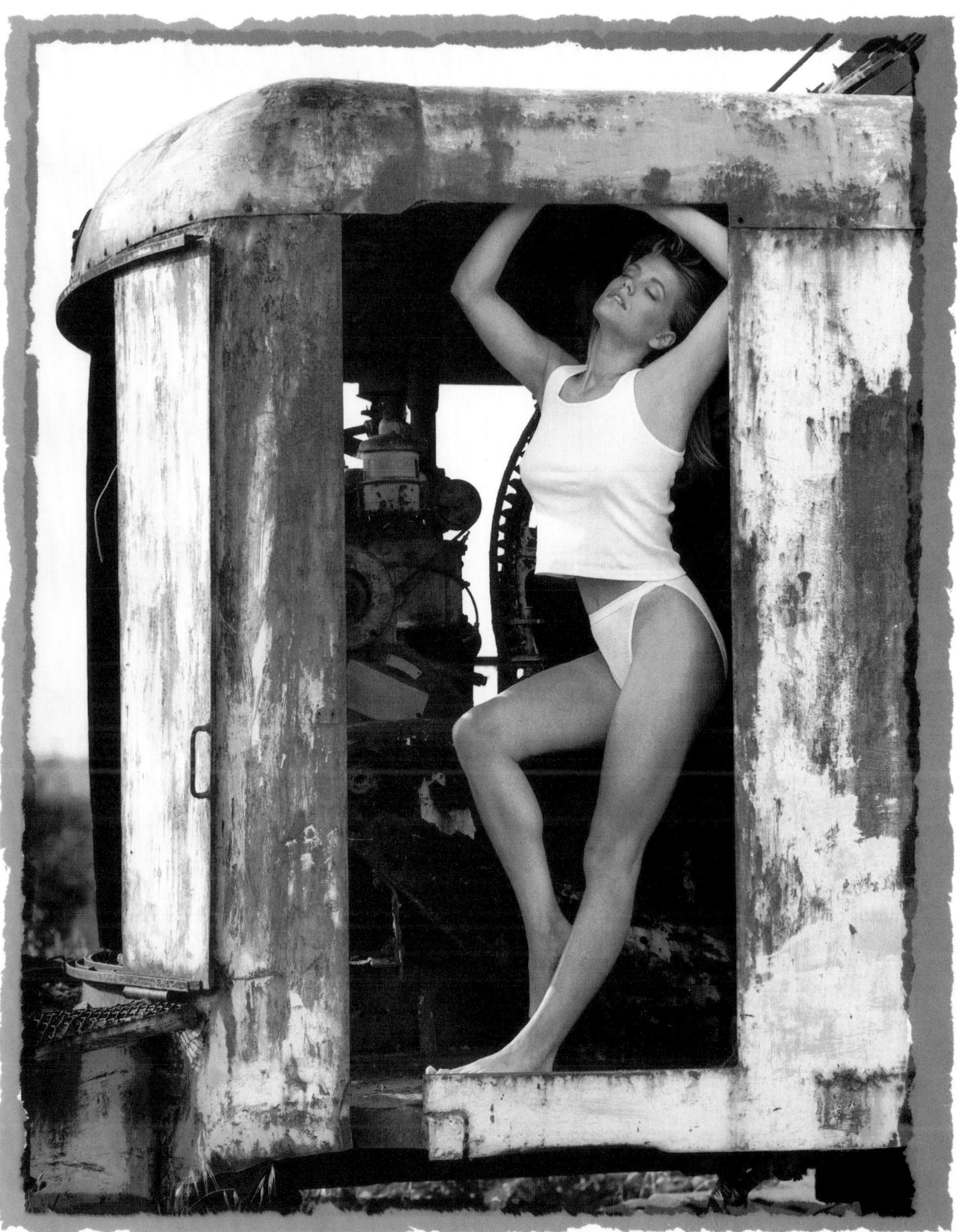

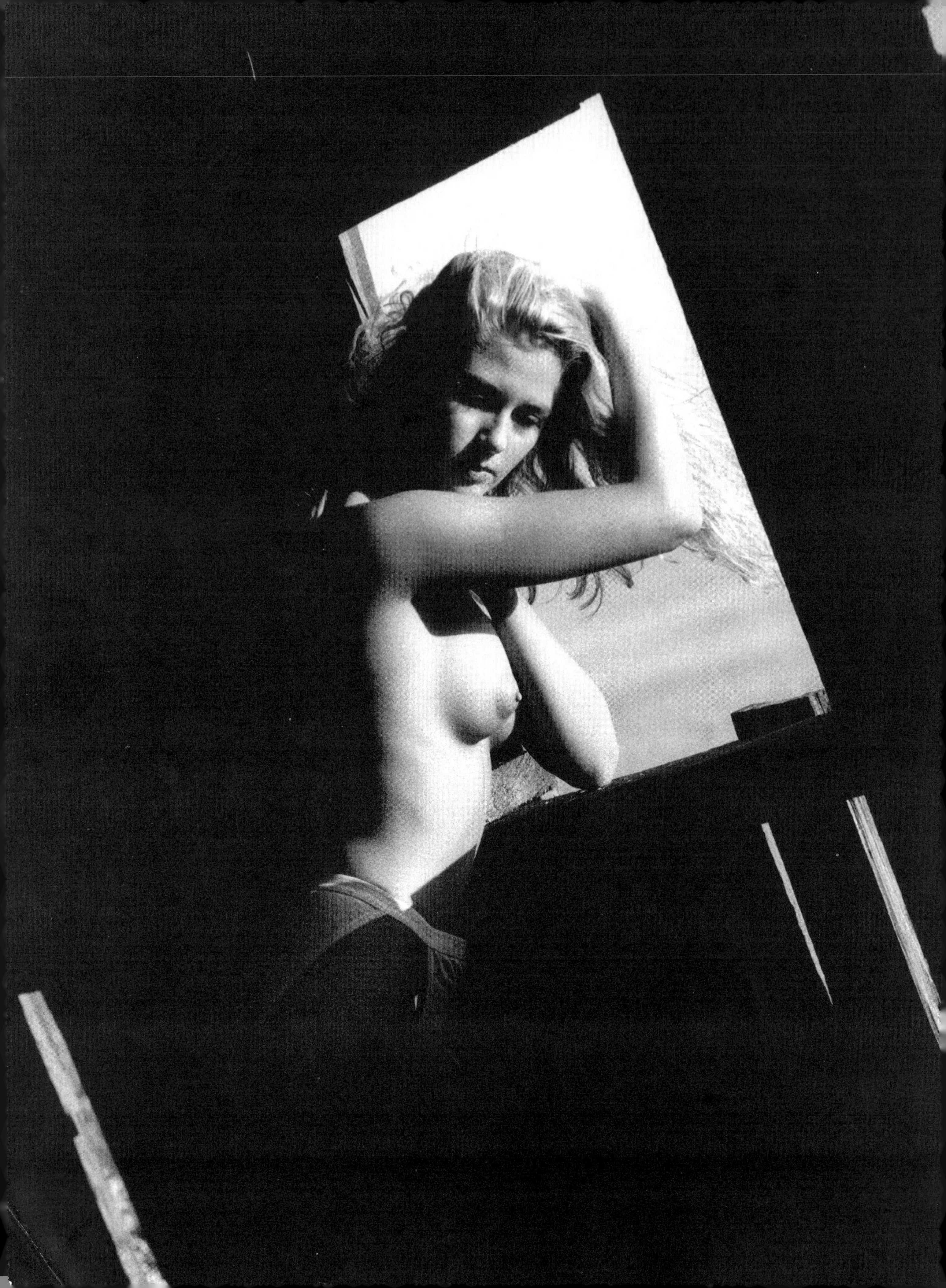

■ Posing

Poses should make models look natural and relaxed. Therefore, it's a good idea to keep your eyes open, and watch how your model moves and sits and behaves when she's not in front of the camera. For example, I shot this image on the spur of the moment when I noticed the model leaning on a windowsill and pulling back her hair. The soft, natural pose in this beautiful light was just too good to pass up.

■ Wind

Weather conditions can be frustrating on location. Wind can limit your ability to use natural light and particular poses because it tosses your model's hair in the way. Occasionally, you'll simply have to give up and reschedule.

Still, wind can sometimes be used to your advantage. In this image, the model's hair was caught by a light wind as she leaned toward the window. The movement of her hair adds motion to the entire image.

"The soft, natural pose in this beautiful light was just too good to pass up."

CAMERA
Nikon 8008
LENS
300mm
FILM
Kodak TMZ 3200 rated at 1600
LIGHTING
natural
MODEL
Dale Colman

■ Posing

This image was created at the barn in which I created many of these images. The model is seated on the back stoop with one leg in the barn and one leg out. Although she is leaning quite far forward, the tilt of the camera makes her look as though she is sitting straight up.

■ Lighting

The model is positioned so that the noon sun, streaming in through the door, illuminates her hair and breasts. A good amount of shadow balances these bright spots. Notice, too, that the light coming in from behind her defines her left breast. Without this area of light, the dark bra could have blended in with the shadowy background.

■ Natural Light

Although the light used is all natural, it is still used very consciously. Using natural light doesn't mean that you give up the opportunity to manipulate light effects. Lighting consists of two elements: sources and surfaces. With natural light one must focus on controlling the surfaces, rather that the sources. This is accomplished by arranging the model in the light, rather than by arranging the light around the model. It is a challenging task, but one which can yield tremendous results.

BILL LEMON'S HINTS AND TIPS:
Learning to use natural light effectively can be a good investment in time for photographers shooting in areas where it is inconvenient to transport large quantities of equipment. It is also a worthwhile study for those who don't use assistants on location and therefore lack the "extra hands" often required to make efficient use of complex lighting set-ups.

CAMERA
Nikon F3
LENS
80-200mm
FILM
Kodak TMZ 3200 rated at 1600
LIGHTING
natural
MODEL
Lalanya Hudspeth

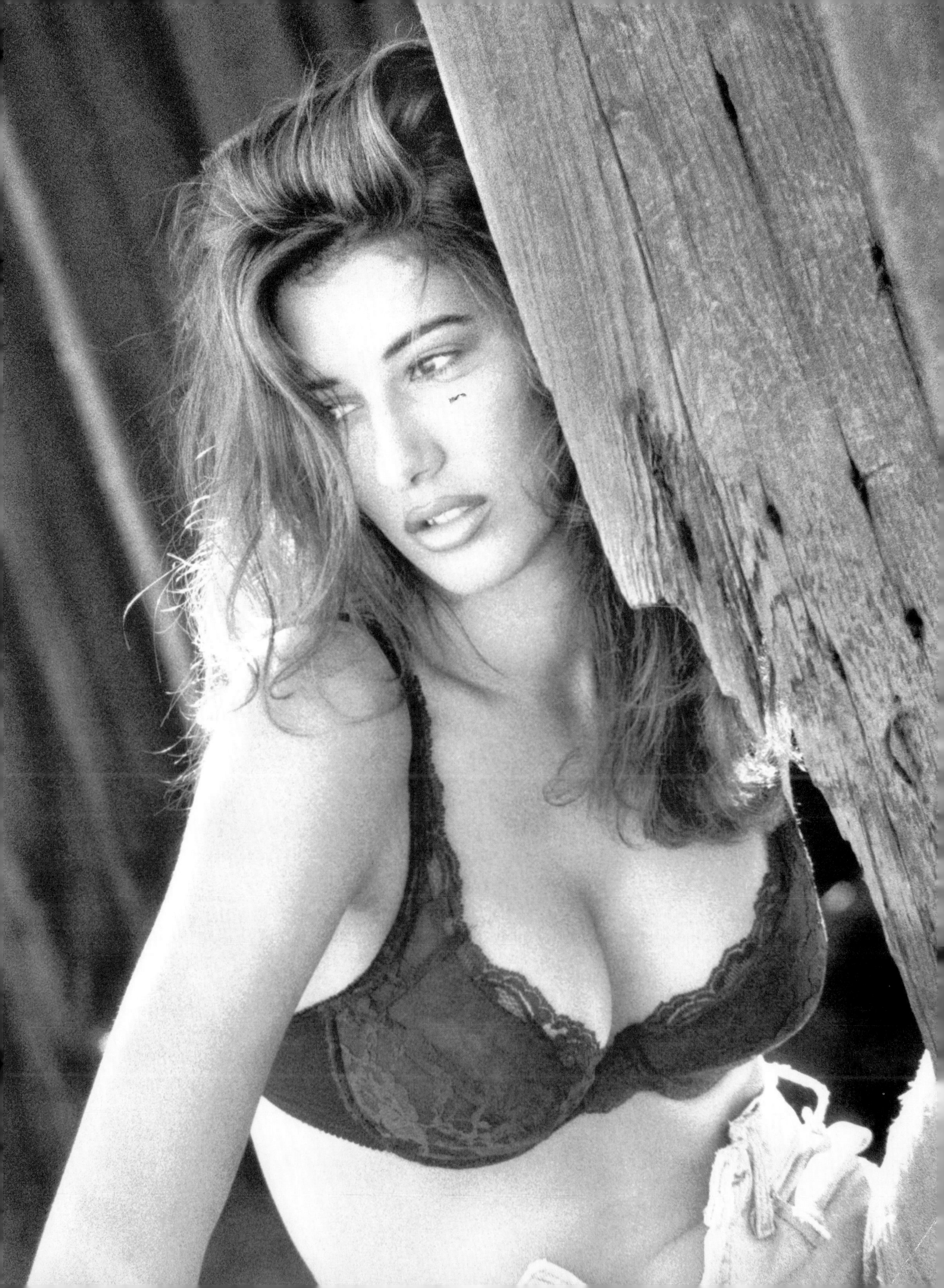

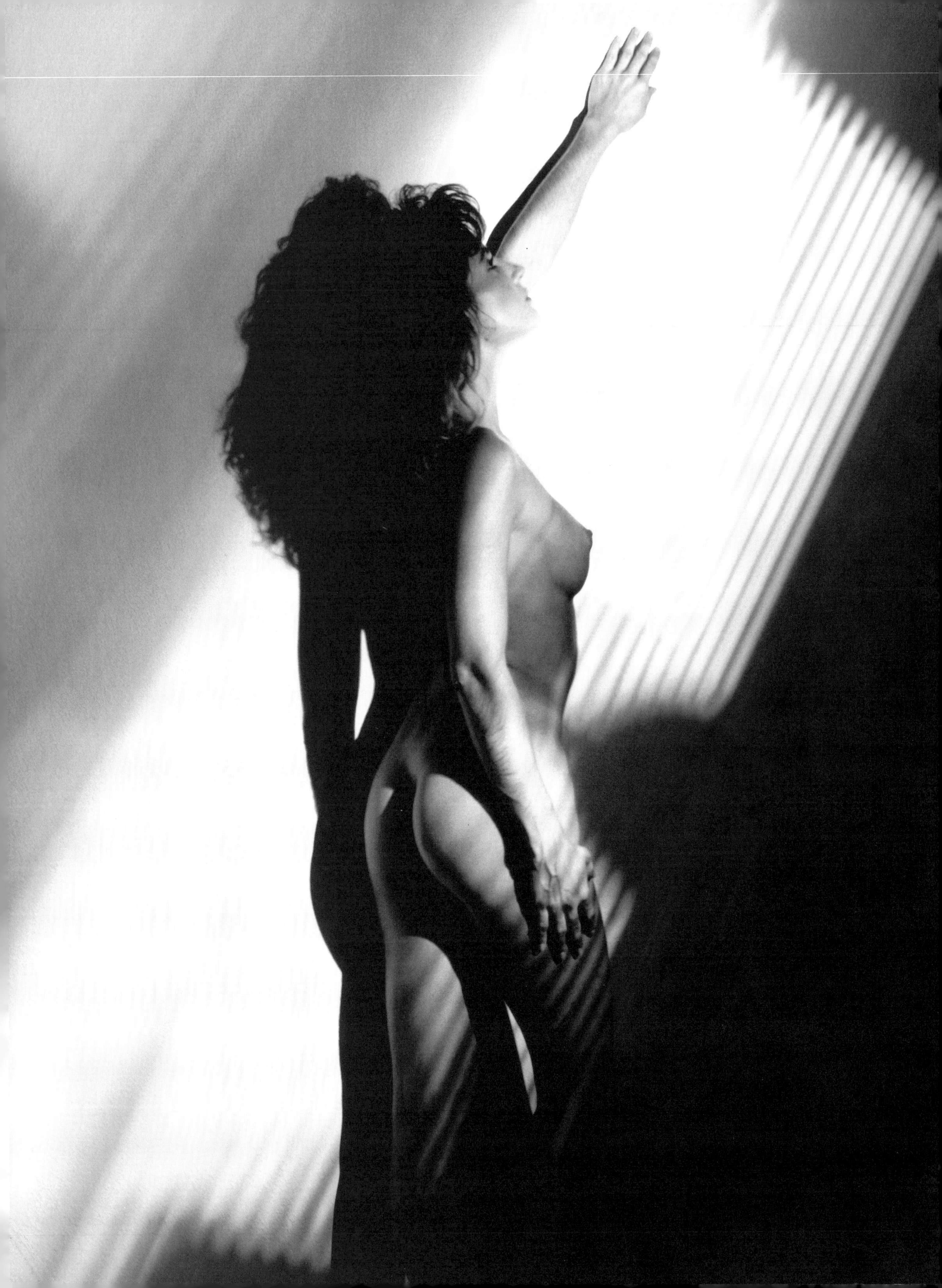

■ Lighting

The lighting used in this shot was something I came upon entirely by accident. I had been working with this model in another area of my studio when the phone rang. When I went to answer the phone, I noticed the interesting pattern of light coming from the side of a grid spot on a strobe head. Keeping your eyes open for light opportunities can be as beneficial in artificial light as it is in natural.

The major focal points in this image are created by the strong light on the model. Notice the sharp, dark shadow behind her, the way her torso is framed in the central light area, and the shadowy silhouette of her breast.

■ Posing

The model's pose in this image was geared specifically to the lighting. Her left arm is lifted, and her head is tilted, to match the angle of the line of light falling all around her.

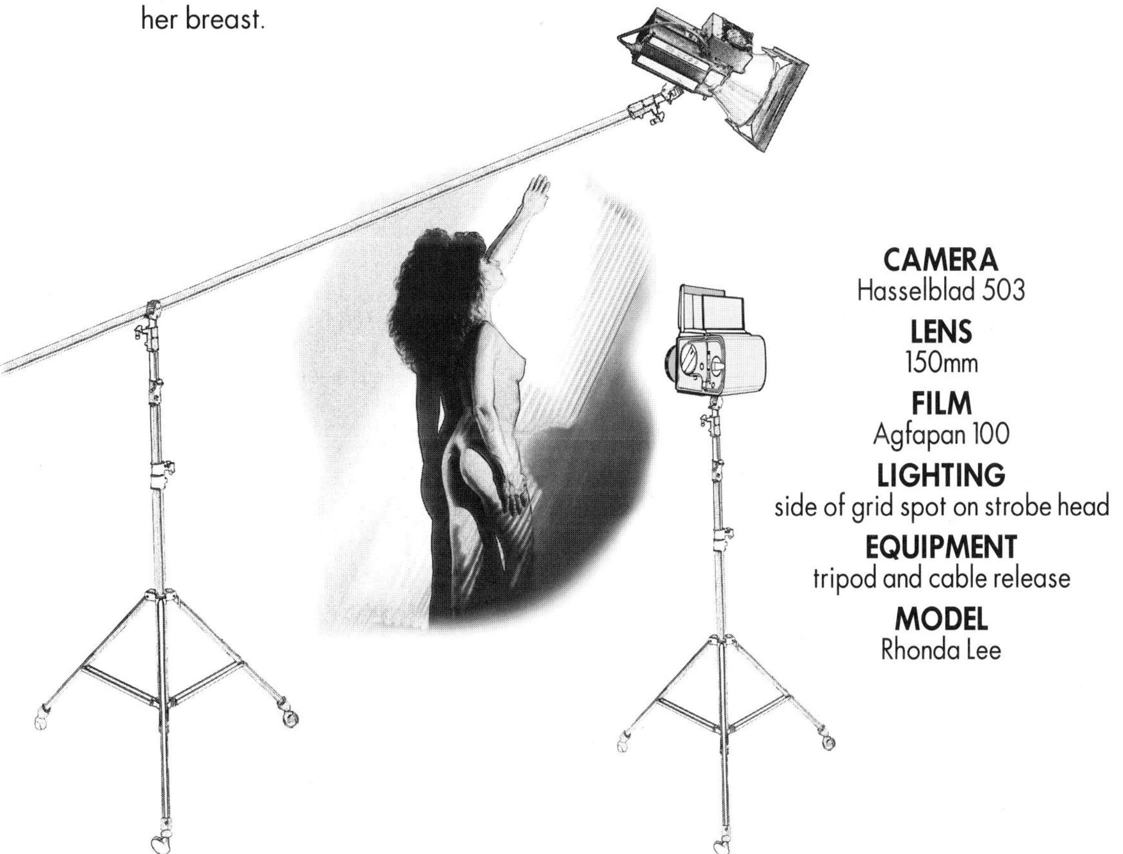

CAMERA
Hasselblad 503
LENS
150mm
FILM
Agfapan 100
LIGHTING
side of grid spot on strobe head
EQUIPMENT
tripod and cable release
MODEL
Rhonda Lee

■ Posing

This image is a good example of why its important not to give up on a particular pose if it doesn't work out the first time. Before shooting the image, I had also tried to shoot it with the model wearing a see-through long sleeve teddy. The image just didn't work that way, and really needed to be done nude.

The pose itself is flattering, and emphasizes the curves of the model's body (especially the curve of her left hip) in contrast with the rigid vertical lines all around her in the barn. The tilt of the camera also emphasizes this curve.

■ Model Selection

The image contains many light tones (the model's skin, the bright white light behind her), so the model had to have dark hair and facial features to make this image successful. The same image with a blonde model would still be beautiful, but would lack the drama of this image.

■ Film

Selecting Kodak TMZ 3200 and rating it at 1600 is what creates the slight grain in this image. The effect is extremely soft and makes the model's skin look absolutely flawless.

"The effect is extremely soft and makes the model's skin look absolutely flawless."

CAMERA
Nikon F3

LENS
80-200mm

FILM
Kodak TMZ 3200 rated at 1600

LIGHTING
natural

MODEL
Nenna Quinn

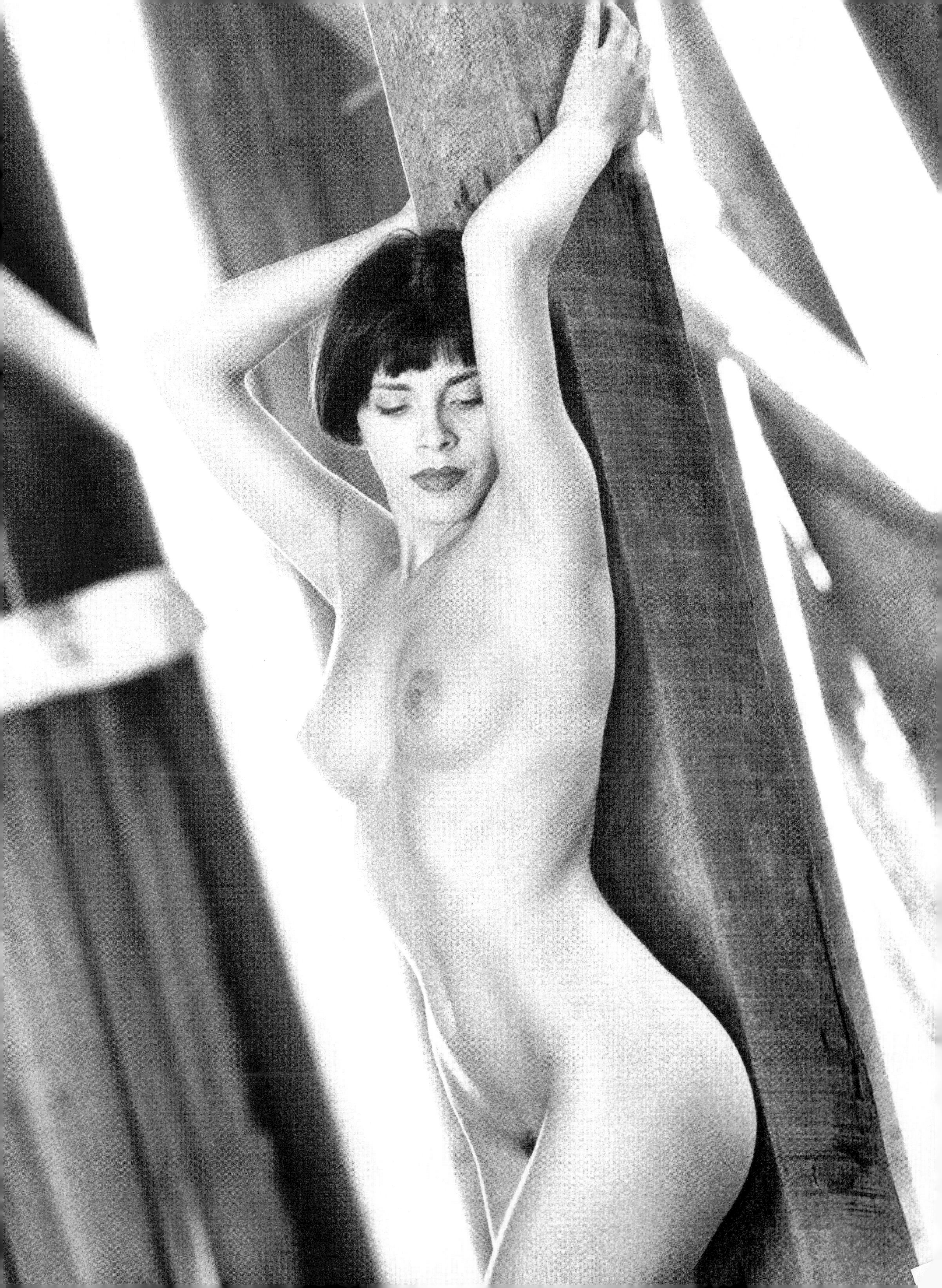

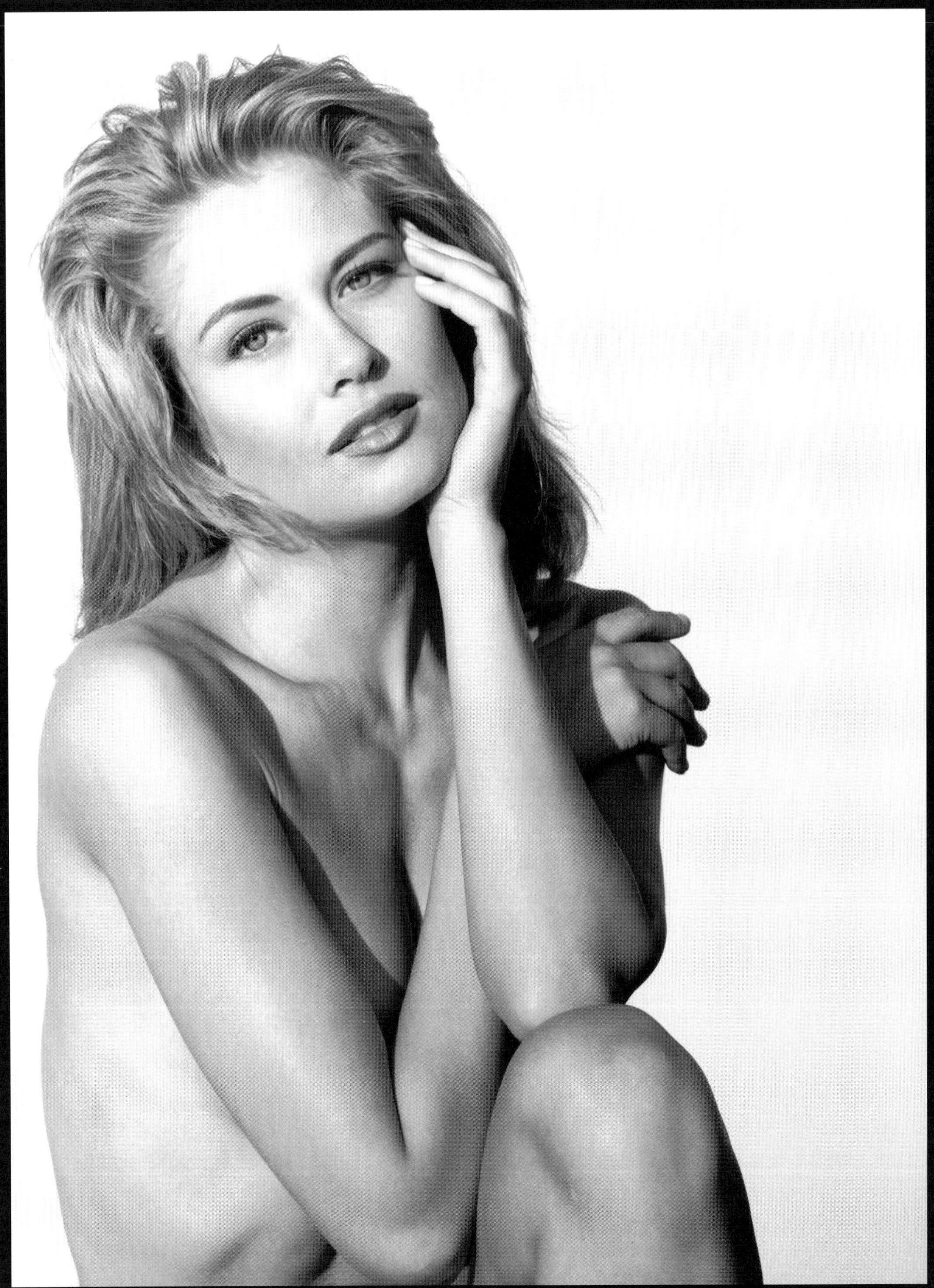

■ Exposure

For this image I selected Kodak TMX 100 because I find it does a good job of catching skin tones. Shooting the image at *f*16 also makes every bit of the image here very sharp.

■ Lighting

The model here was photographed in late afternoon sun. She faced west and the sun was behind the camera. Her head is tipped up slightly to catch the full effect of the sun.

■ Posing

Although she looks completely relaxed, the model here was actually balanced strategically on a 10″ wide tractor tire. Her pose, although nude, is sensual without being revealing. The soft fold of her arms is very feminine and makes her look natural and comfortable

CAMERA
Hasselblad 503
LENS
150mm
FILM
Kodak TMX 100
LIGHTING
natural
MODEL
Dale Colman

■ Setting

This image was photographed in a white shower stall, with lighting bounced off the ceiling onto the model. It required me to shoot into the shower from atop a chair. The addition of water to an image can be very powerful. The droplets on her lips and body make her skin look sensual.

■ Cropping

The photograph was cropped rather tightly. Cropping can be a great tool, but be careful not to go overboard with it. It was important for the composition to keep the model's left elbow in the frame. Her arms frame the center of the scene and accentuate the curves of her neck and breast. This is accentuated by the printed border on the image.

■ Light and Shade

With a white shower stall and a nude model, this image could easily have been a little too light. Notice, however, that while the overall photograph contains many light tones, there are still local areas of high contrast (such as between the model's neck and shoulder). This can be achieved by slightly underexposing the image. Including a full range of tones (especially on skin) is something to shoot for in almost every image.

CAMERA
Nikon F3

LENS
24mm

FILM
Kodak TMZ 3200 rated at 1600

LIGHTING
Norman, 200 watt sec.,
bounced off ceiling

MODEL
Kirsten Bucheister

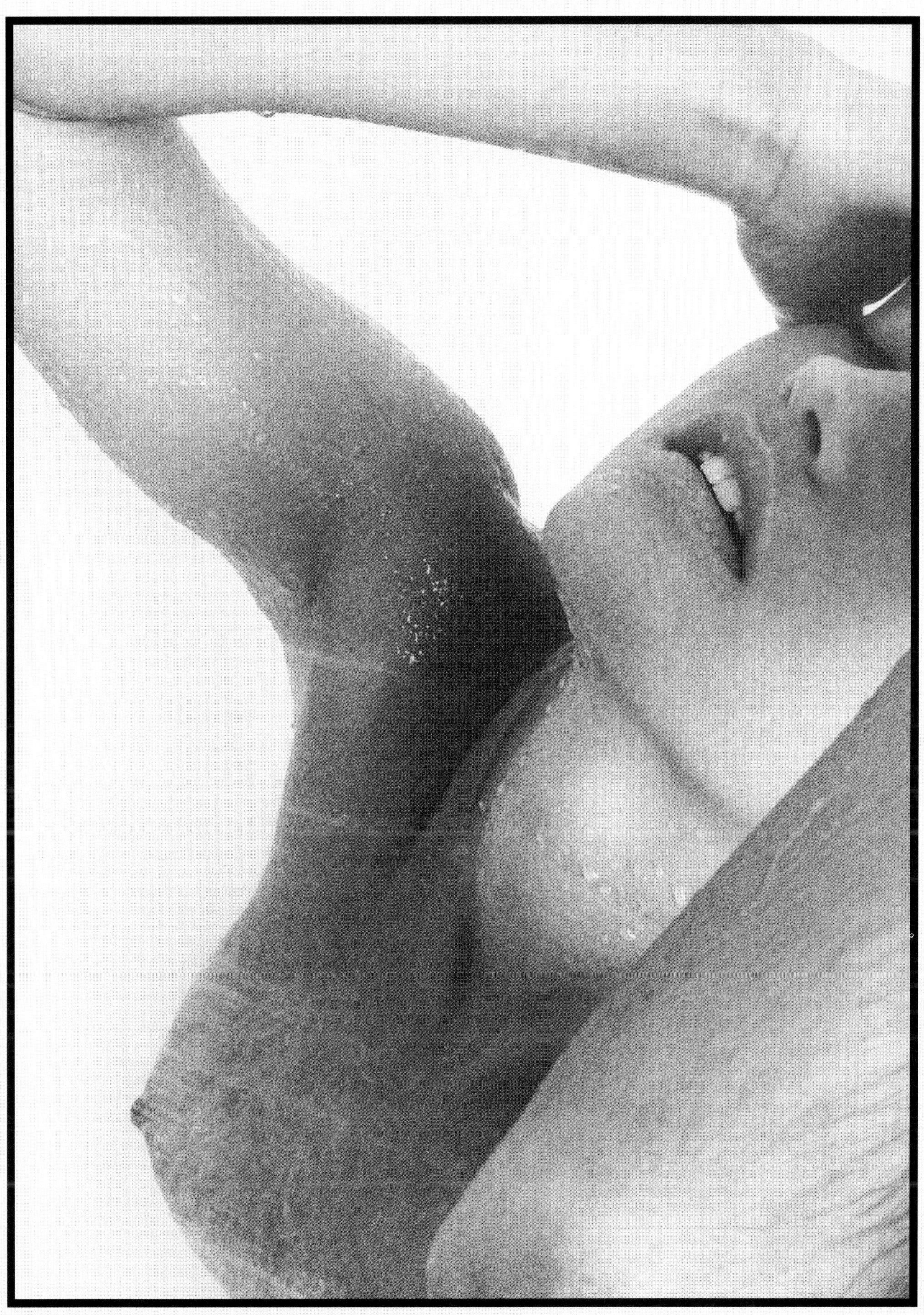

■ Setting

The model here is posed leaning against the side of an old crane. The rust and paint on the old metal really make the model stand out nicely from her surroundings. Notice also that the focus is sharply on the model and the background behind her is allowed to go completely soft.

■ Hands

The fold of the hands in this image is a very soft and feminine gesture. One of my rules of thumb is to try never to cut off a models hands when framing an image. Sometimes this rule must be violated, of course, but hands can be very expressive and I find that they usually make an image better.

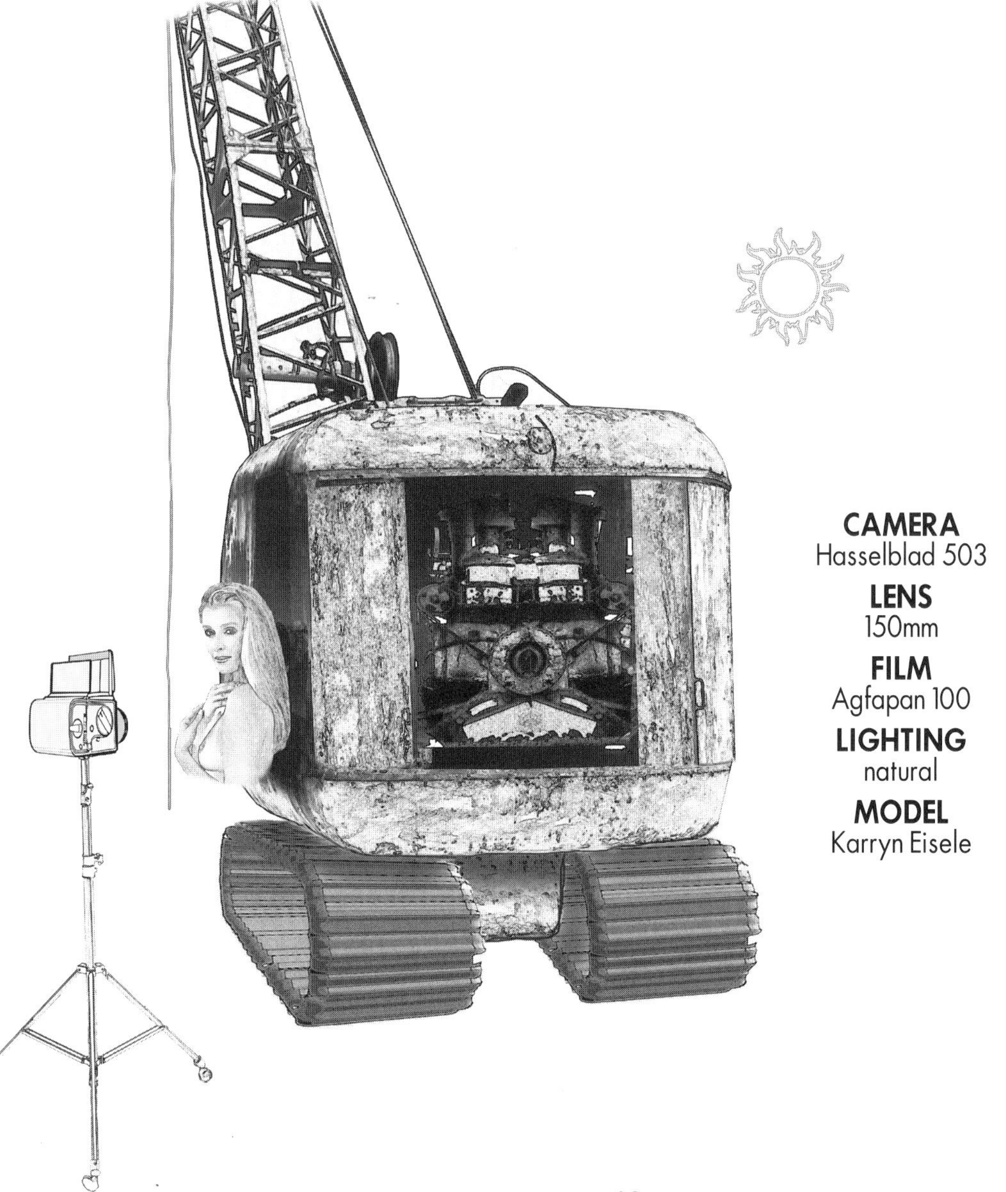

CAMERA
Hasselblad 503

LENS
150mm

FILM
Agfapan 100

LIGHTING
natural

MODEL
Karryn Eisele

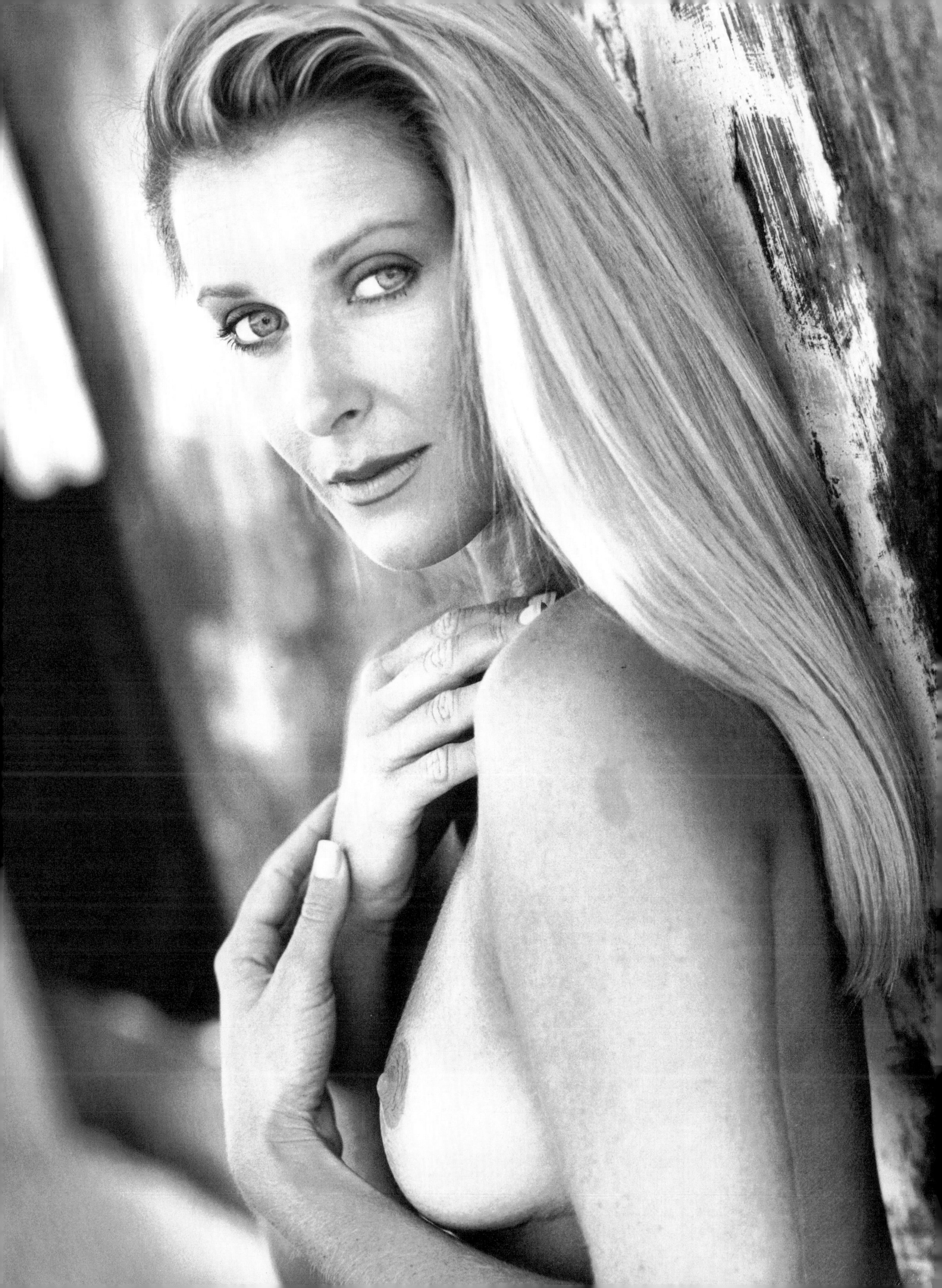

■ Posing

You'll notice that many of the models in this book are posed with their heads tilted far back and their eyes closed. It's both a very sensual pose, and one which is flattering to many models. Additionally, in a shot like this one where the model's face is not the focal point of the image, it helps to accentuate the upper body by lengthening and revealing the neck and upper chest.

This image demonstrates the fact that creating a sensual image isn't just about nudity. Here, the model reveals no more than she would in a one-piece bathing suit, but the pose which highlights her bent legs and pulled-down shirt is extremely sexy.

■ Water

This model was photographed in a small stream in Austin,Texas. You'll find several images herein that depict models with damp skin and hair, or being showered with water. It's hard to explain exactly why, but the addition of water to a shot almost instantly increases its sensuality.

"...the addition of this element to a shot almost instantly increases its sensuality."

CAMERA
Hasselblad 503
LENS
80mm
FILM
Kodak TMX 100
LIGHTING
natural
MODEL
Lauren Elliot

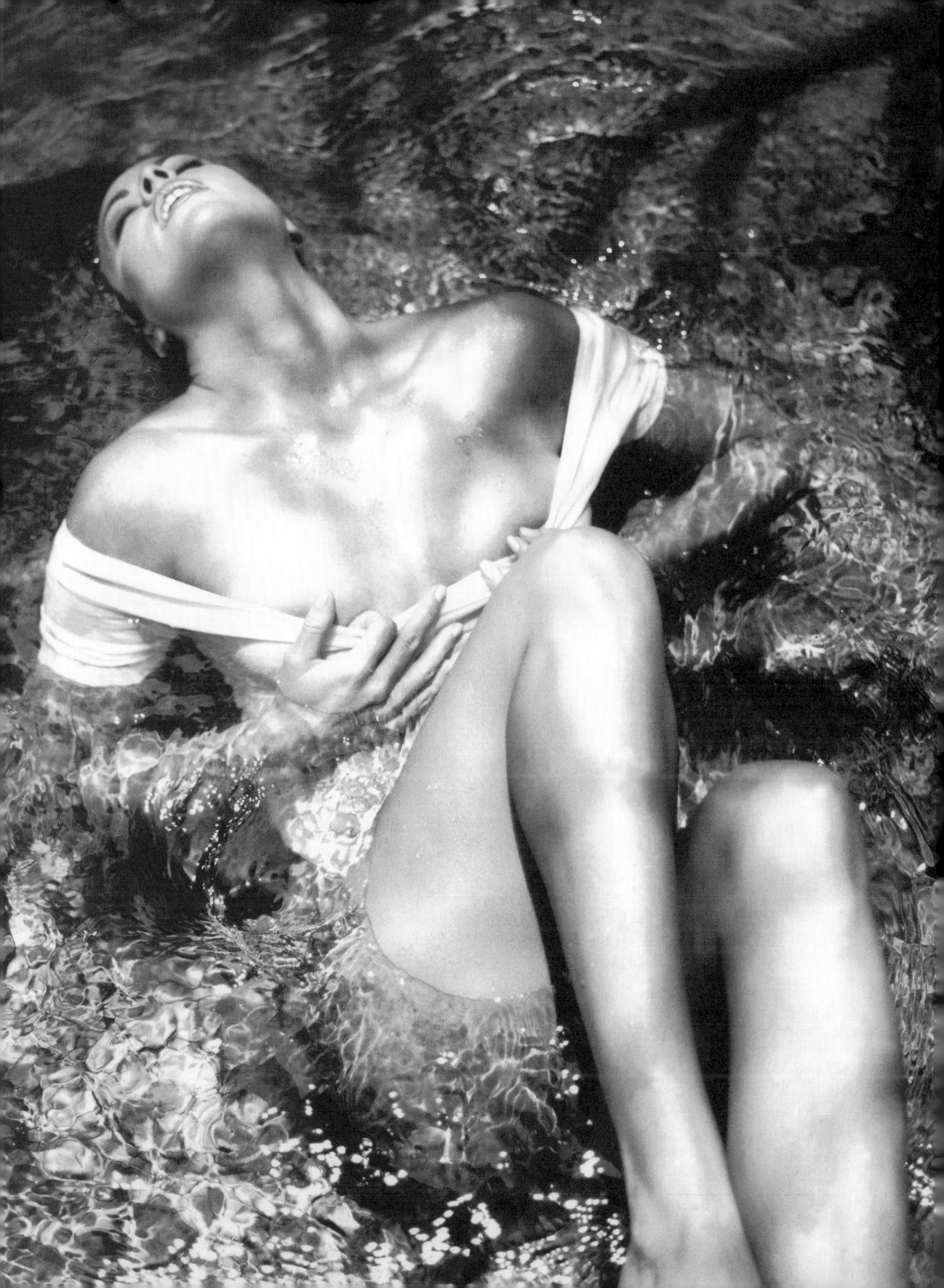

■ Lighting

You can see by the grass at the bottom right corner of this image that the light was extremely hot when this photograph was shot. Because if this, it was important to position the model in shade — provided here by some old gasoline tanks. A scrim further softened the illumination coming in from the left-hand side of the image.

■ Composition

Always placing the subject in the center can get boring. The rule of thirds can be a helpful technique for creating balanced images, though it won't work for every shot. Here, by framing the model off to the right-hand side of the image, it became possible to include more of her legs, an important component of the photograph.

■ Clothing

The selection of this button-down white cotton tank shirt was important. Because the shadows behind the model are very dark, the white of this shirt helps to focus the eye on her body and brings it out of the shadows.

"The light was also controlled by placing a scrim ..."

CAMERA
Hasselblad 503
LENS
150mm
FILM
Kodak TMX 100
LIGHTING
39"x39" scrim
MODEL
Kirsten Bucheister

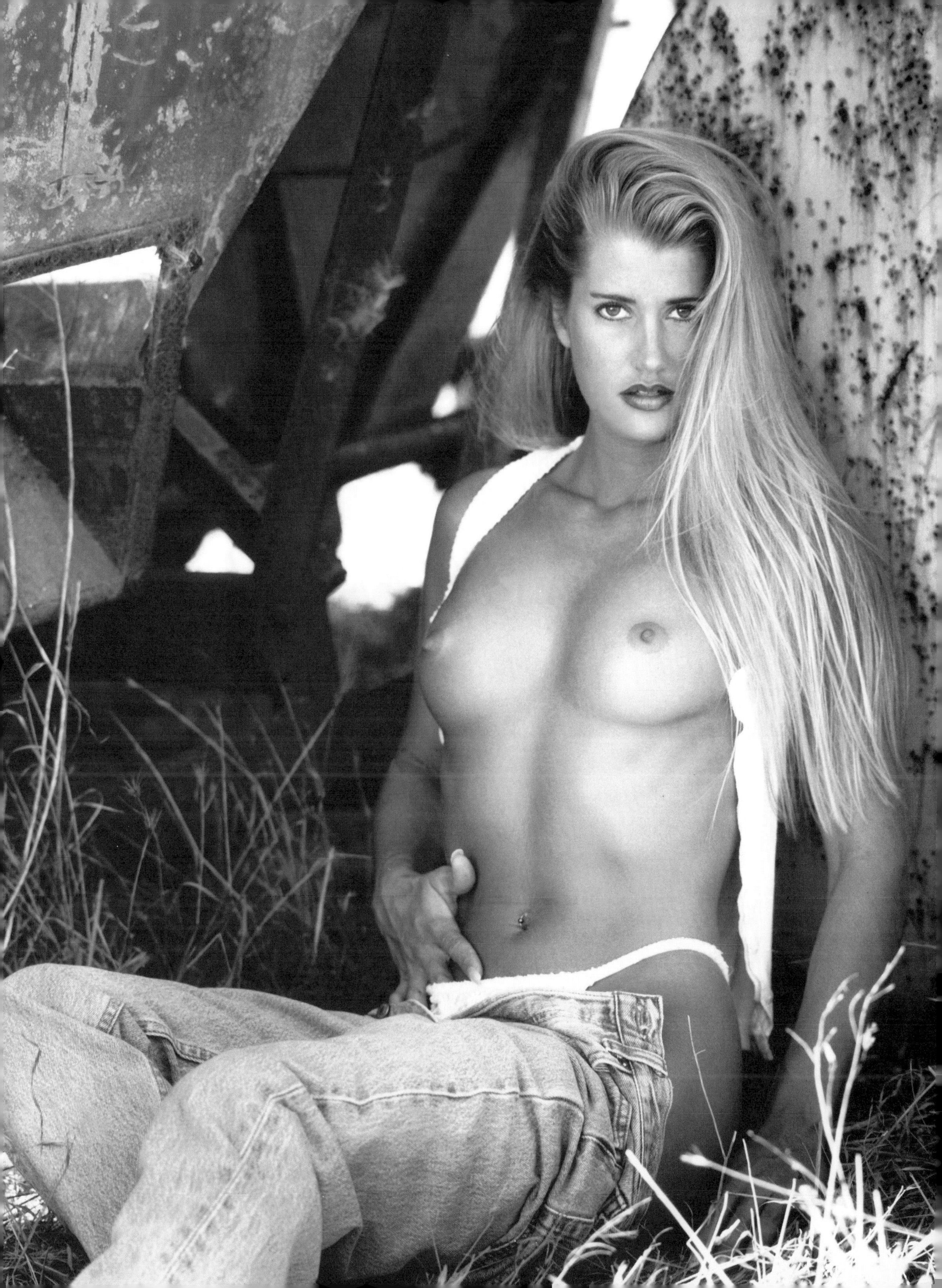

■ Lighting

With some images, timing is everything. This is especially true when using natural light. Inside a structure the sun may only hit the ideal spot at certain times of day or at certain times of the year. For this image, we had to be in the barn late in the afternoon to catch the right light. About two months after the image was taken, the sun angle had changed sufficiently that the natural light was no longer good for repeating this shot.

■ Posing

This pose is obviously a good one for emphasizing beautiful legs. The uplift of her arms lifts her breasts and makes the whole image more appealing.

■ Composition

Here, centering the model in the frame creates a dramatic impression that is emphasized by the crossbeams on the barn behind her. These beams act like beacons, focussing the eye in on the model's body. A dark garment was chosen to match the overall darkness of the image; white would have been too stark in this setting.

BILL LEMON'S HINTS AND TIPS:
Light conditions in one area can change profoundly with the time of day, the season and the weather. While this can mean that a shot that works in the summer won't in the winter, keep in mind it also means that with each new season and hour, new lighting becomes available. An image that didn't work at noon may suddenly be possible at five in the afternoon.

CAMERA
Hasselblad 503

LENS
150mm

FILM
Agfapan 100

LIGHTING
natural

EQUIPMENT
tripod and cable release

MODEL
Annette McKnight

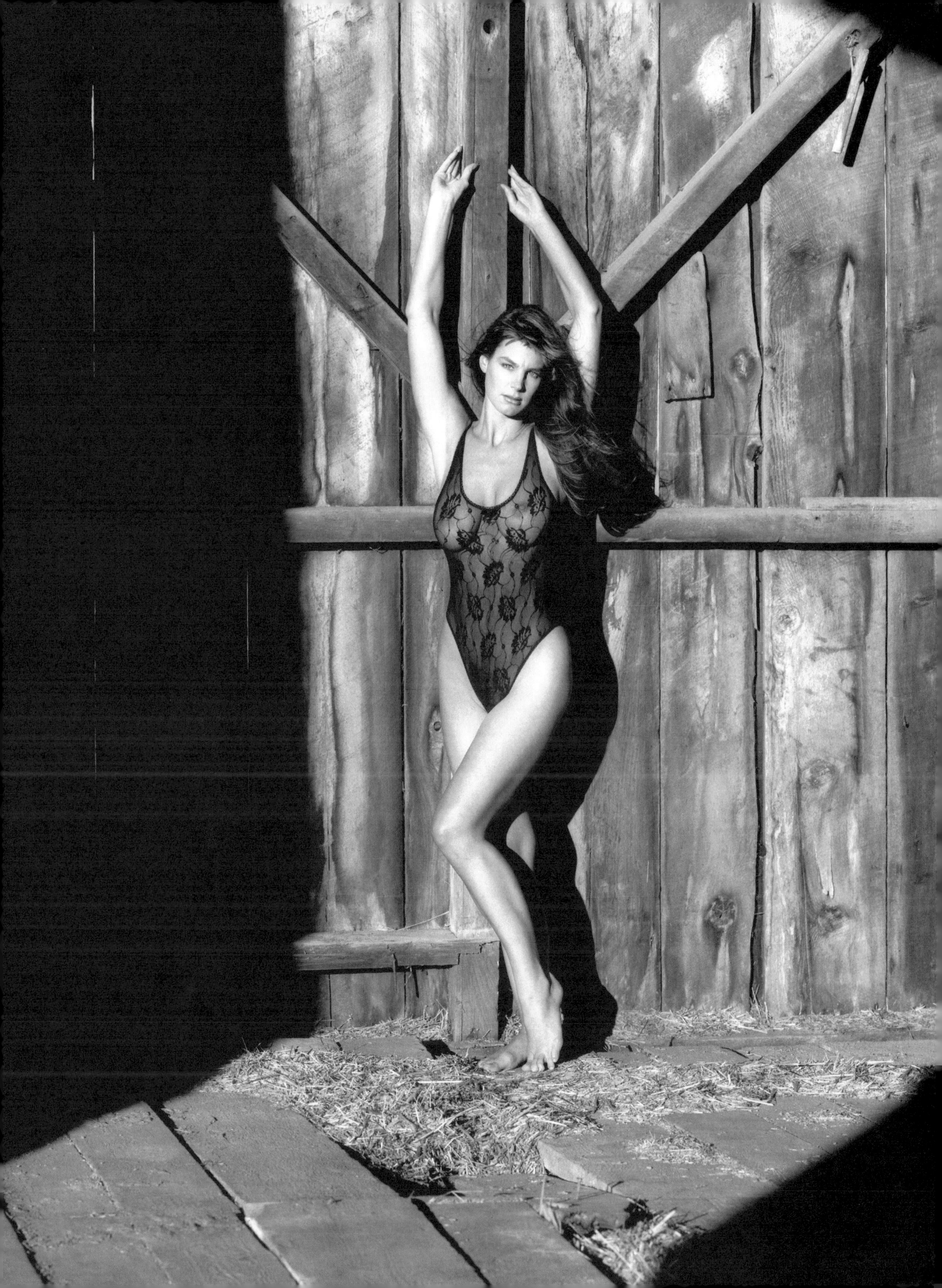

■ Model Selection

Just as you may find one setting that just works really well for you, you will also probably find that some models suit your style better than others do.

Physical appearance isn't the only thing that counts when looking for models. The personality, attitude and energy a model brings to a shoot can be just as important to the quality of the final images as the equipment you bring. With one model you may have to spend a long time just to get one good image, with others you can reliably come home from a shoot with many great images. When I find a model, such as this one, with whom I get consistently good results, I try to use her a lot.

■ Posing

This image was taken with the model sitting on the back of a rusty old crane. Her left knee is lifted and her right leg is extended straight out. The late afternoon sun, almost at sunset, creates beautiful light and shade relationships on her body and emphasizes the skin tones and softness of the image. Still, it is strong enough to vibrantly illuminate her face and the left side of her body.

"...some models suit your style better than others do."

CAMERA
Hasselblad 503
LENS
150mm
FILM
Agfapan 100
LIGHTING
natural
MODEL
Jane Sanquinetti

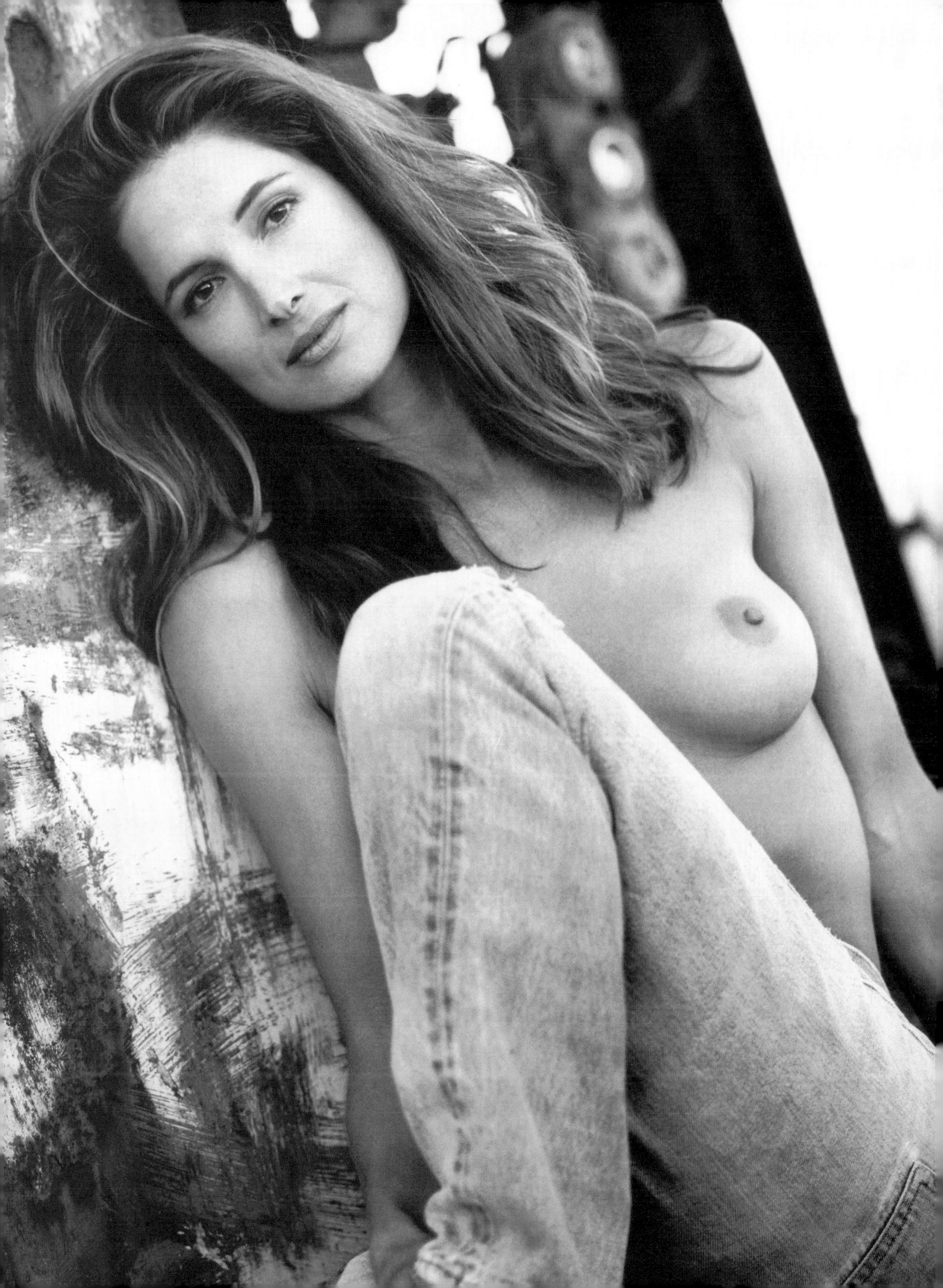

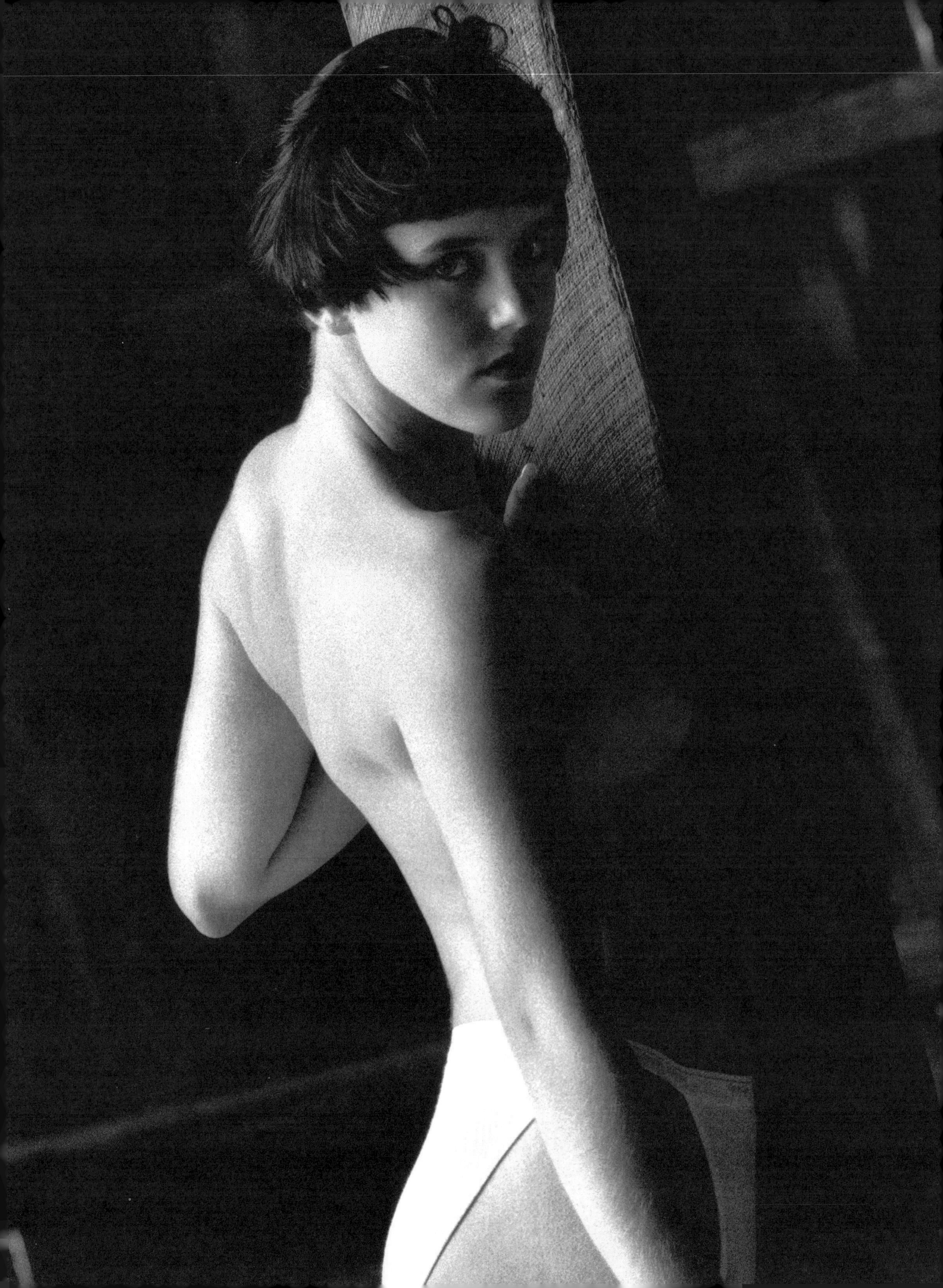

■ Printing

This is one of my favorite images, and one that has turned out to be very versatile. I have had it printed several different ways since I originally shot the photograph. Some lighter prints have been made of the image to show more of the front of her body, and some have been made darker to hide it. The one pictured here is in the mid-range of these.

■ Model Selection

This is an image where model selection was important. This model's short, dark hair complements the overall tone of the image in a way that long, blonde hair simply would not.

■ Posing

In this image I broke my rule about not cutting off hands, but here, it works. The model was photographed inside the barn next to a post (the texture of which shows up well with this film and rating). I took the light reading off her back, rather than her face, because this was to be the emphasized part of the image. Still, the small amount of light coming between her body and the post shows her face in beautiful profile.

"This model's short, dark hair complements the overall tone of the image..."

CAMERA
Nikon F3

LENS
180mm

FILM
Kodak TMZ 3200 rated at 1600

LIGHTING
natural

MODEL
Coleen Zimmerman

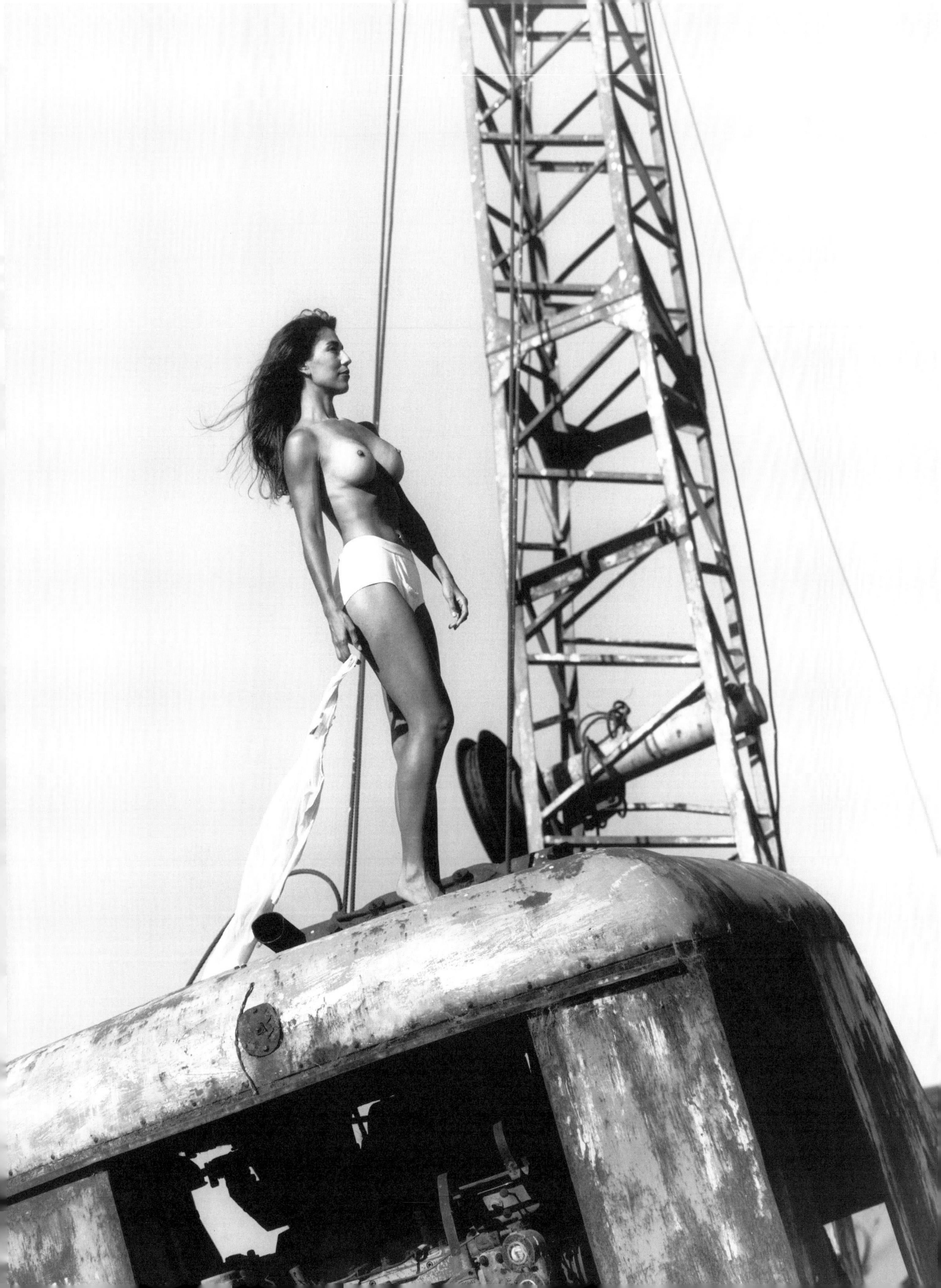

■ Setting

The barn in which so many of these images were shot is extremely private, which is important for doing any nude or semi-nude work. It presents a vast array of textures and settings in which to pose the models. Still, I hadn't really exploited the full potential of the location until one summer when the barn was full of bees and wasn't safe to use. This situation forced me to begin to think more creatively about the other features of the spot, such as the old agricultural equipment around the barn. I discovered that the textures and lines of equipment, like this crane, also offered as many possibilities as the barn itself for the creative photographer.

■ Posing

This model's powerful looking body is perfectly situated on top of the old crane, which itself looks powerful and strong. Rather than the soft, feminine lingerie of many of the other images, this model is shown wearing men's briefs.

■ Camera Tilt

Here, as in many of the images, a slight tilt of the camera adds dimension to the image. The angle is subtle, but the effect on the image is powerful.

"This situation made me begin to think creatively about the other features of the spot..."

CAMERA
Hasselblad 503
LENS
150mm
FILM
Agfapan 25
LIGHTING
natural
MODEL
Athena Chavarria

■ Posing

This image was shot with a very low camera angle so that the line of the horizon behind the model wouldn't seem to cut her body in half, as it would have if shooting from shoulder height. Whether shooting on location or in the studio, it's important to use caution when positioning horizontal elements in the background. These should never intersect with the model's body at the waist, neck or eyes, where they are extremely distracting and make the model look "cut up."

■ Clothing

Different models will want different kinds of images. It's important for a photographer to keep the model's desires and comfort level in mind when preparing for a shoot. One way for you to gauge the situation is by going through your portfolio with the model before you photograph her. See what kind of images appeal to her, and evaluate which poses and settings would be the most flattering for her.

"...use caution when positioning horizontal elements..."

CAMERA
Hasselblad 503
LENS
150mm
FILM
Agfapan 100
LIGHTING
natural
MODEL
Anna Sanchez

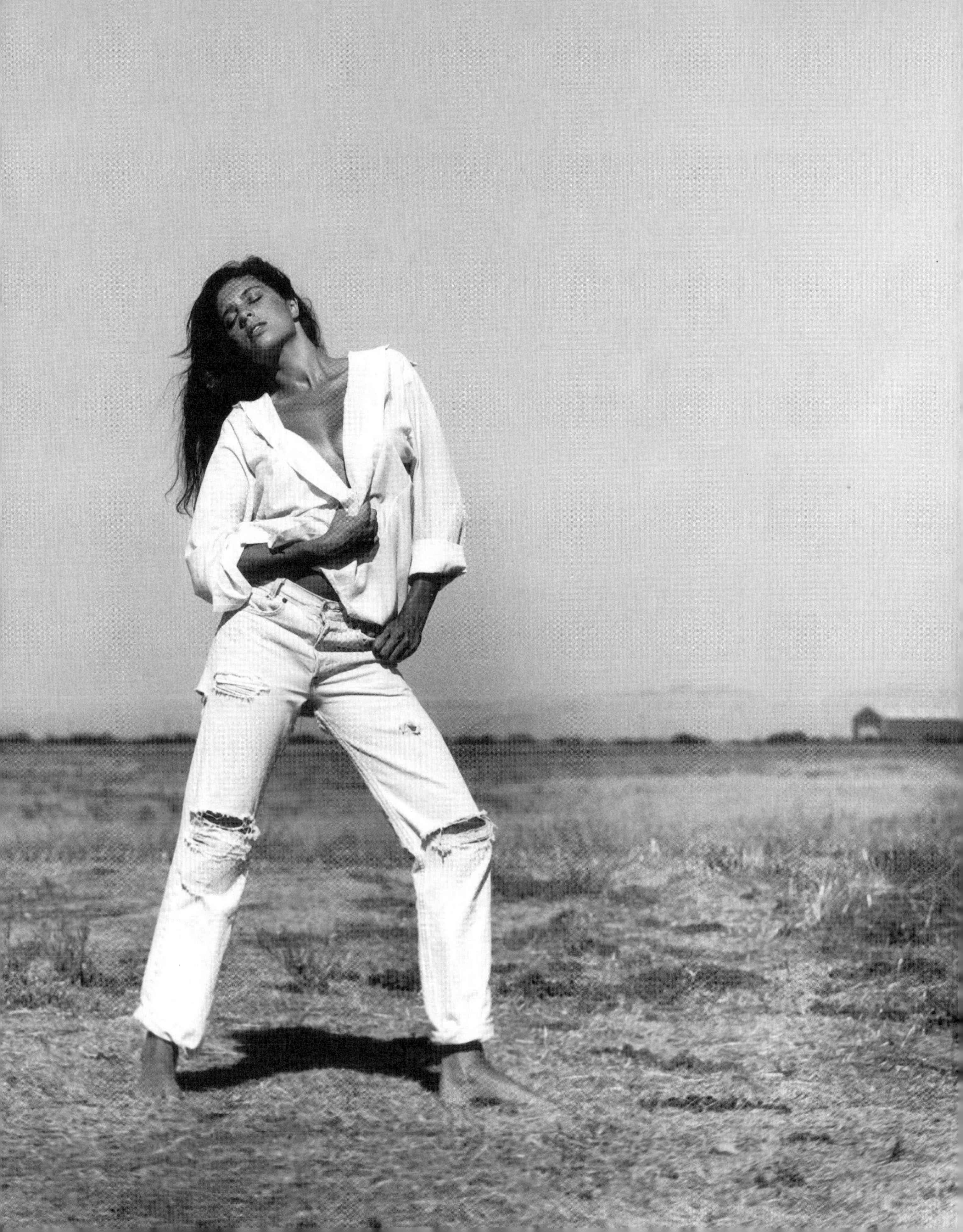

■ Photographer's Comments

Like a couple of other images in this volume, this pose was one that was inspired by the work of Italian photographer Marco Glaviano. I took the image as a sort of experiment because I was interested in learning how the lighting worked in the shot. You can learn a lot by taking the time to consciously practice with light. Starting with an image you like and trying to recreate the lighting used in it can be a very worthwhile exercise, and one that will only increase your efficiency and ability to execute your ideas.

■ Lighting

The lighting effect is very strong in this image, and yet it requires a very small setup. A single light was situated at a 90° angle from the camera, and the lamp was fitted with a single small reflector.

■ Clothing

They may not be a hot fashion item anymore, but tube tops can be a very functional piece of clothing to have on hand. This model did not wish to do a nude session, but by shooting her in a tube top, the effect of a nude shot was created.

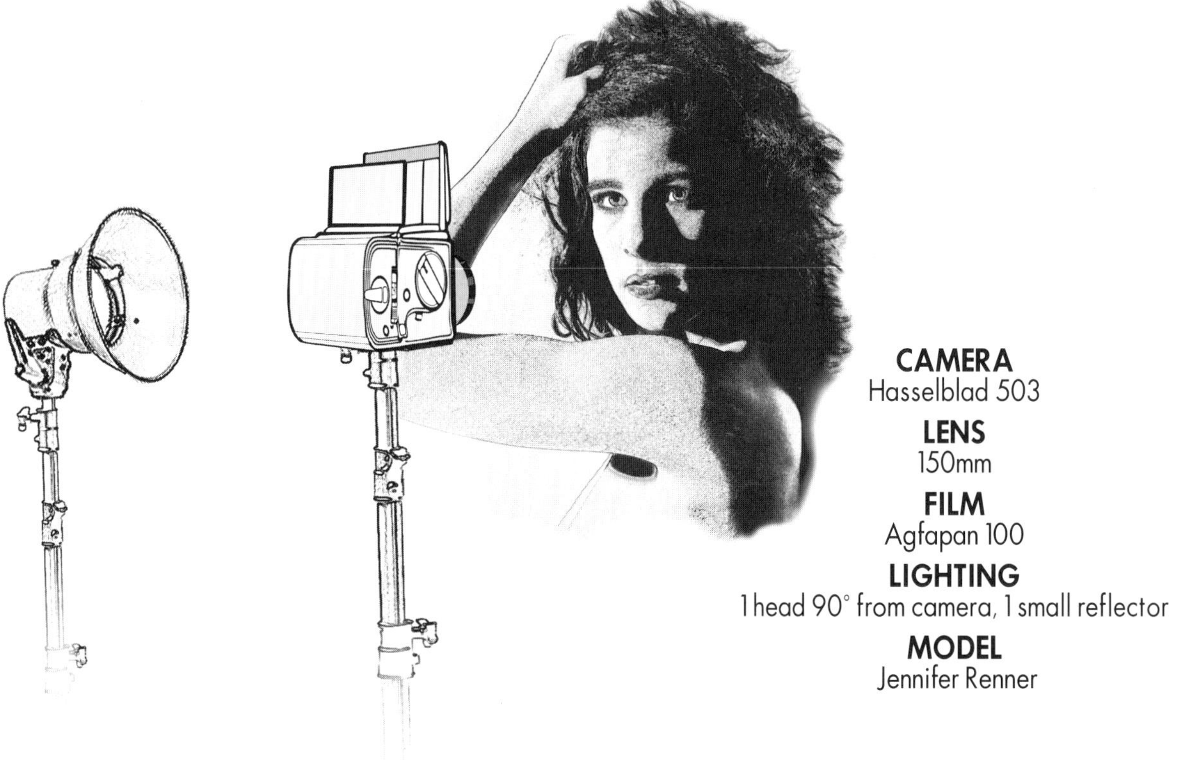

CAMERA
Hasselblad 503
LENS
150mm
FILM
Agfapan 100
LIGHTING
1 head 90° from camera, 1 small reflector
MODEL
Jennifer Renner

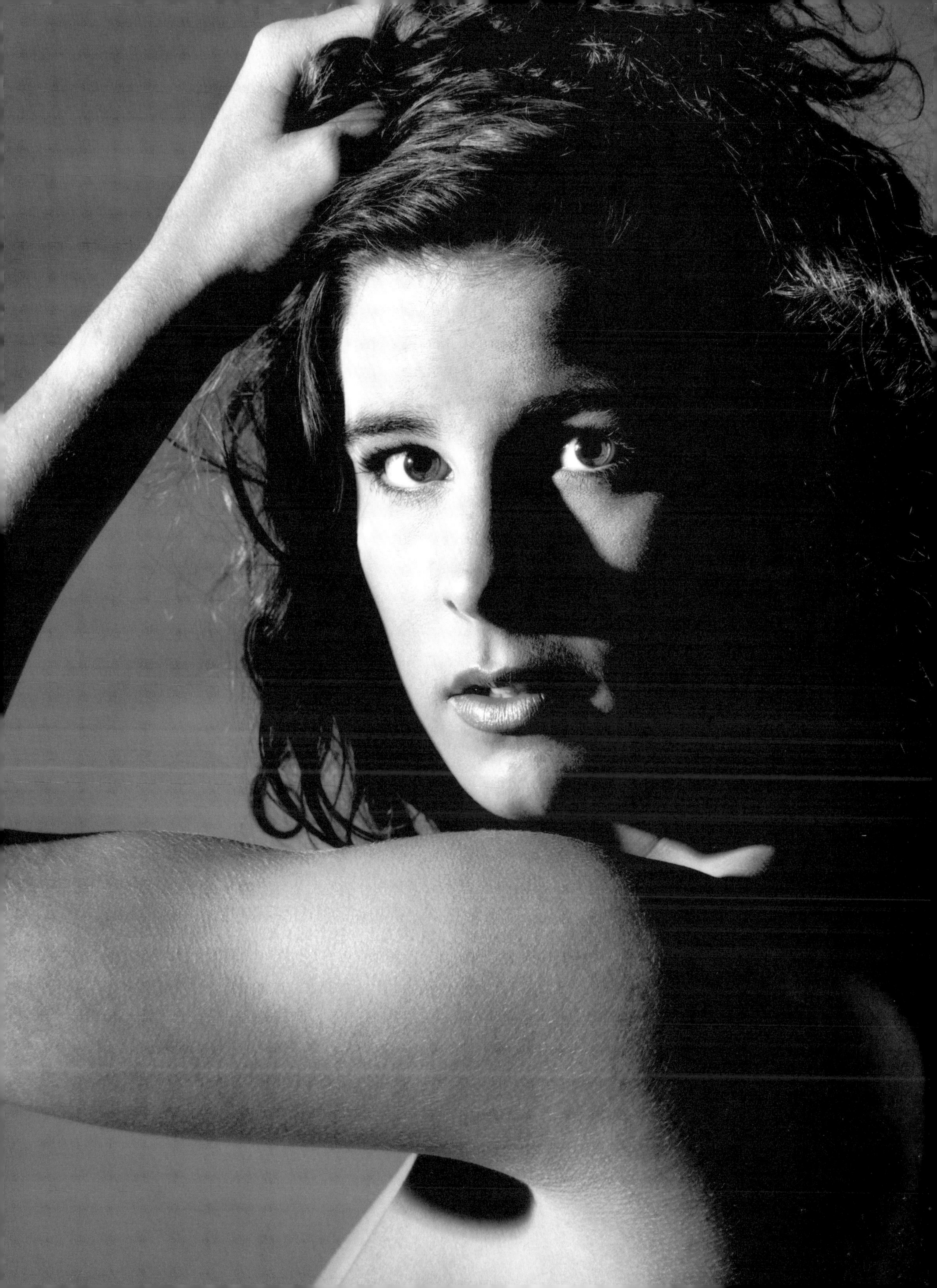

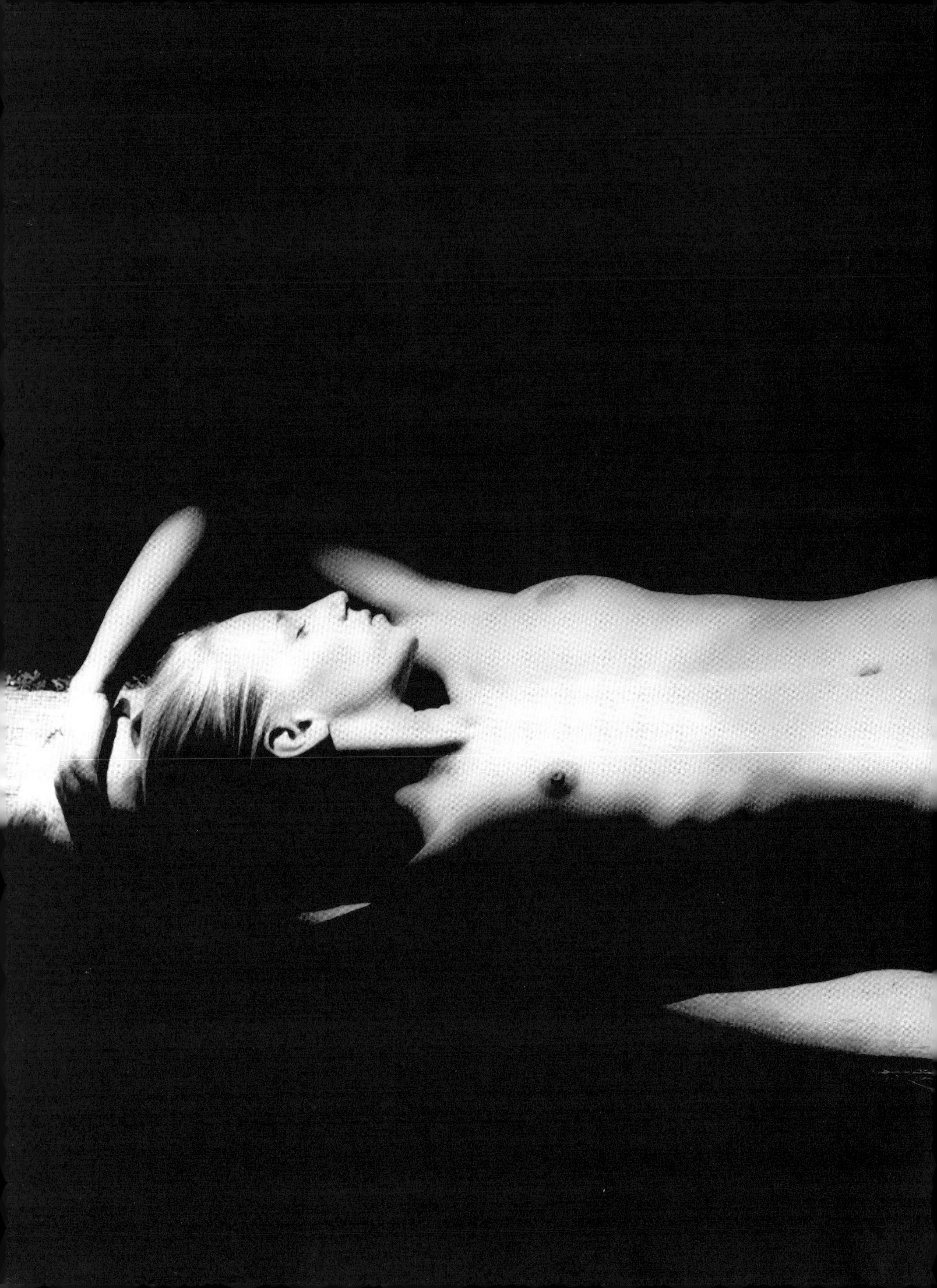

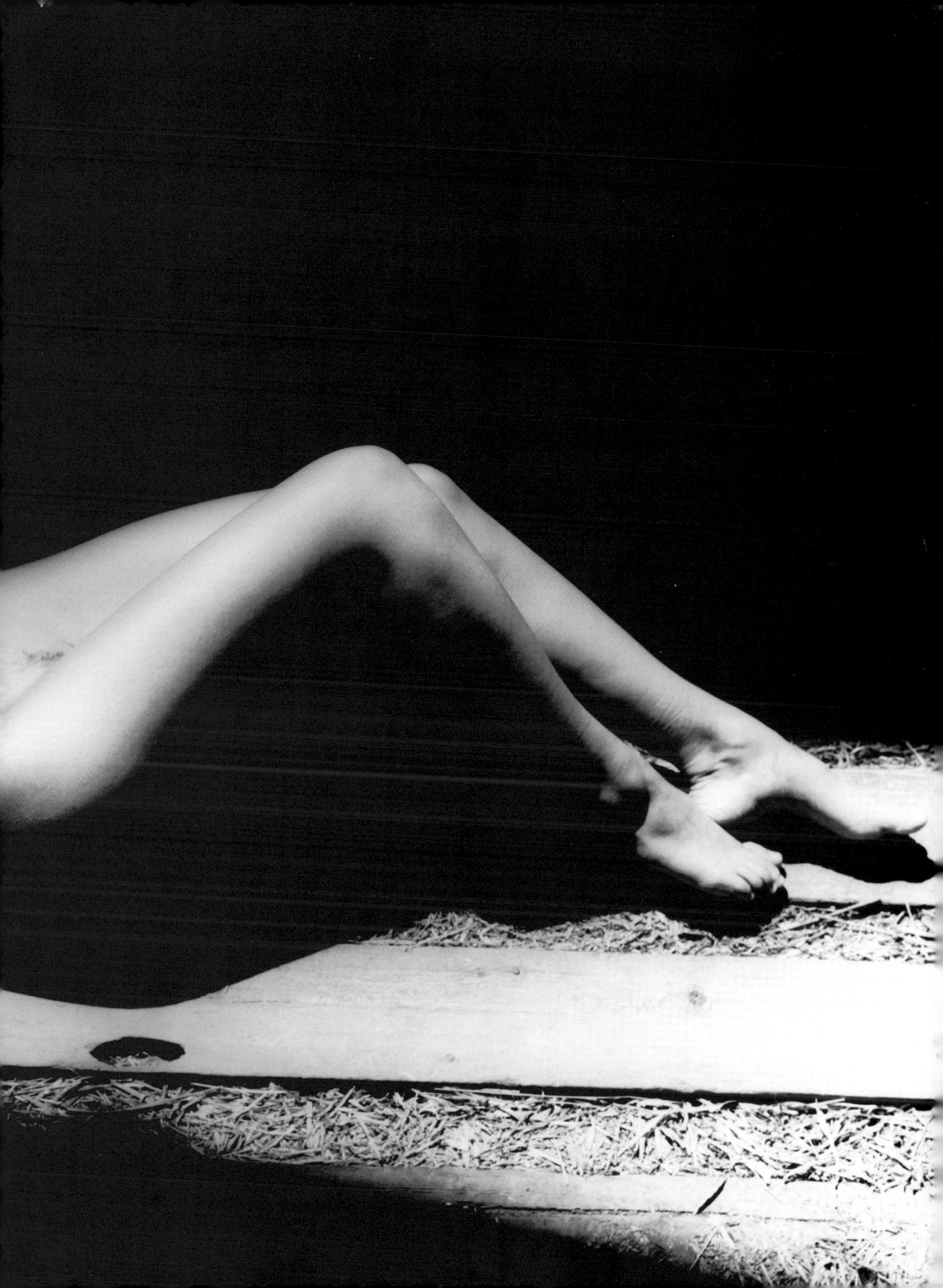

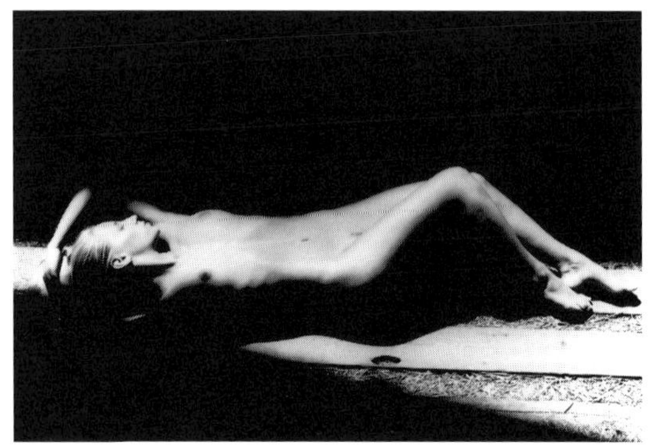

■ Lighting

The lighting in this image comes entirely from the sunlight naturally coming in through the upper back of the barn. Good timing was needed in order to catch the light in this spot, and position the model's body in it. The light reading was taken on the model's face.

■ Setting up the Shot

This image was shot looking down at the model from about a 60° angle. A Bogan super clamp with a Bogan tripod head mounted on it was attached to the top step of a ladder to position the camera properly.

BILL LEMON'S HINTS AND TIPS:
Avoid the temptation to drag your entire studio along with you when going on location, especially if working without an assistant. Instead, learn to use what's there: the natural light features, the existing setting. Thinking creatively about these can both increase the quality of your images and simplify your life!

CAMERA
Hasselblad 503
LENS
80mm
FILM
Kodak TMX 100
LIGHTING
natural
EQUIPMENT
Superclamp, tripod head, cable release
MODEL
Kirsten Harrison

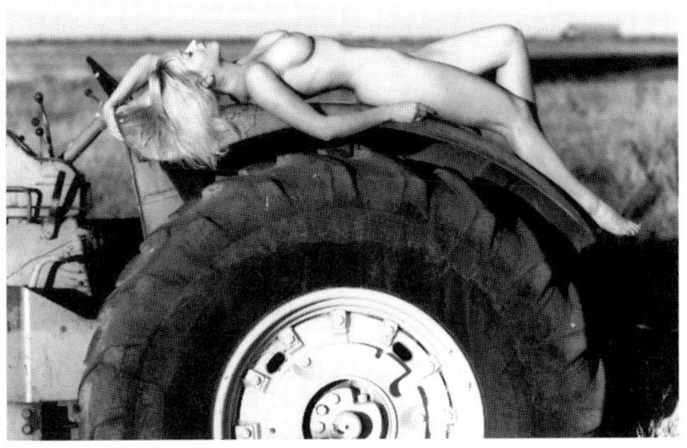

■ Composition

The model's body does not occupy the majority of the frame. Instead, the camera position was lowered in order to fill the image with more of the wheel, and to position her body in the upper part of the photograph. Again, these images are not just about beautiful models, context and contrast play a big part.

■ Setting

When working on location, it's important to keep your mind open and try to keep looking at familiar settings in creative ways. During this shoot, I had been photographing this model sitting on the fender of this old tractor. Suddenly I noticed that her body and the fender were just about the same length. Having noticed that, the pose you see in this image seemed a natural one.

■ Lighting

The late afternoon sun positioned behind the camera illuminates the model from head to toe and makes her skin almost seem to glow.

CAMERA
Hasselblad 503
LENS
150mm
FILM
Kodak TMX 100
LIGHTING
natural
EQUIPMENT
tripod and cable release
MODEL
Malinka

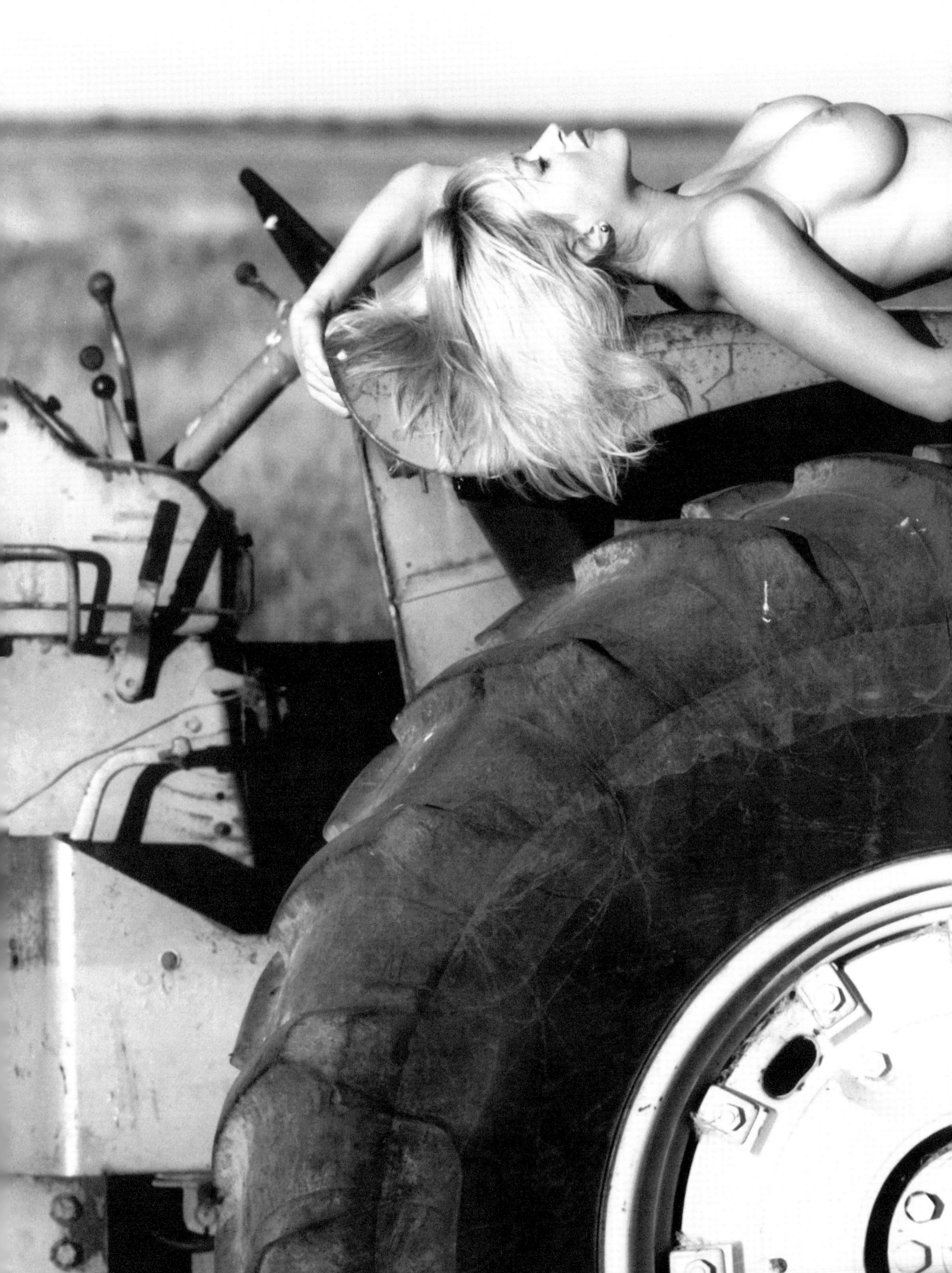

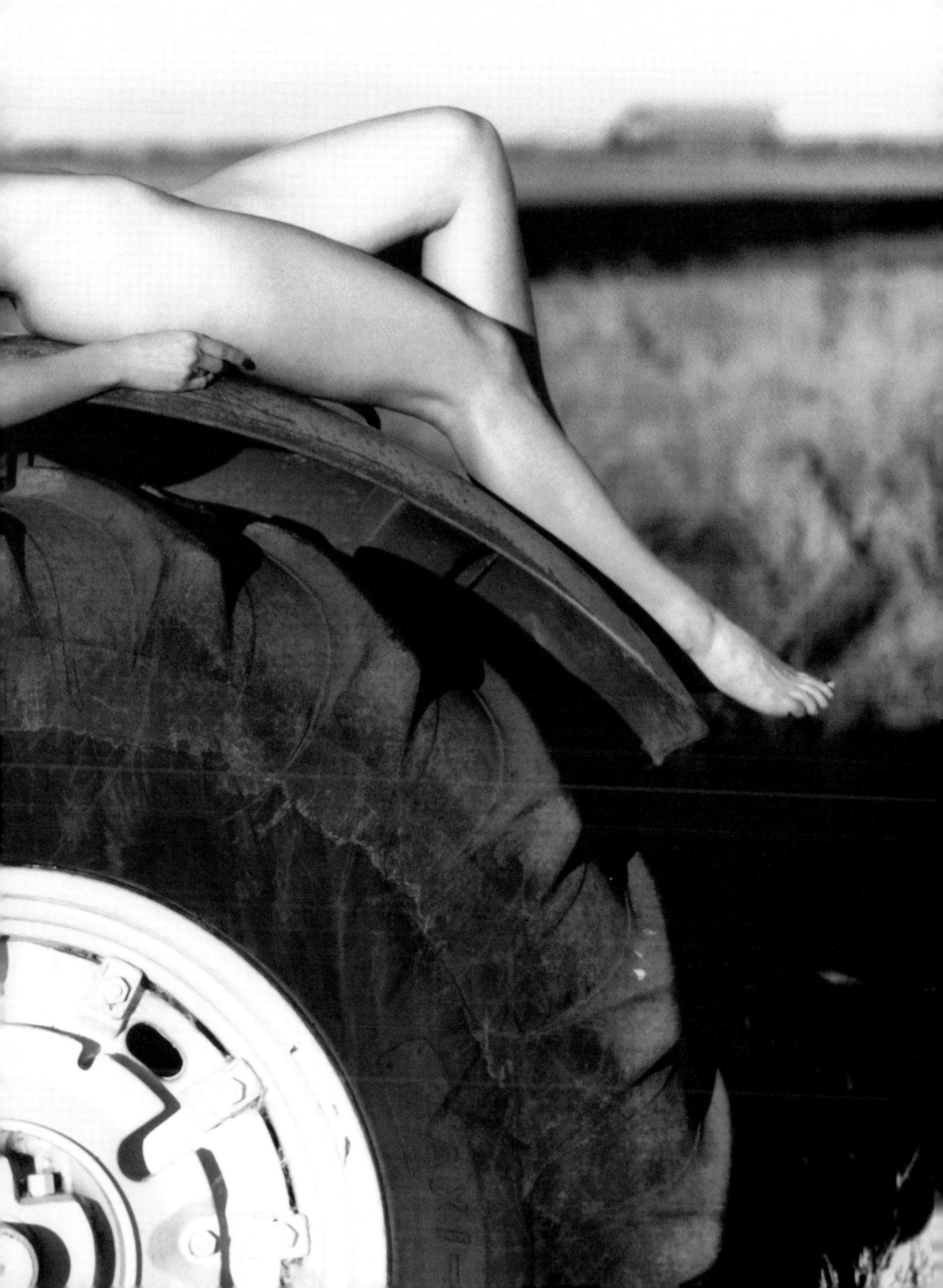

■ Finding Models

One way of finding models is to conduct a model search. I have had success finding models by putting out flyers at local beauty salons, high schools and colleges. It's a good idea to set a lower age limit of about fourteen. Potential models pay a set fee (decided by you) for a photo shoot with professionally done make-up, and one 8"x10" print. The winning model receives the grand prize (perhaps a cash prize, another photo session or an introduction to a modeling agency). I usually find one or two good models through each search. Model searches aren't something you can do every month or even every year. You'll probably want to space them out at intervals of two or three years, unless your markets constantly expand and change.

■ Photographer's Comments

This image was taken about ten feet inside the front door of the barn where there is always good light. It's a spot I find I use over and over again because I never strike out there. The light streams in from the north and creates extremely flattering effects for the skin, eyes and mouth.

"...extremely flattering effects for the skin, eyes and mouth."

CAMERA
Pentax 6x7

LENS
200mm

FILM
Kodak Plus X 125

LIGHTING
natural

EQUIPMENT
tripod and cable release

MODEL
Michelle Piper

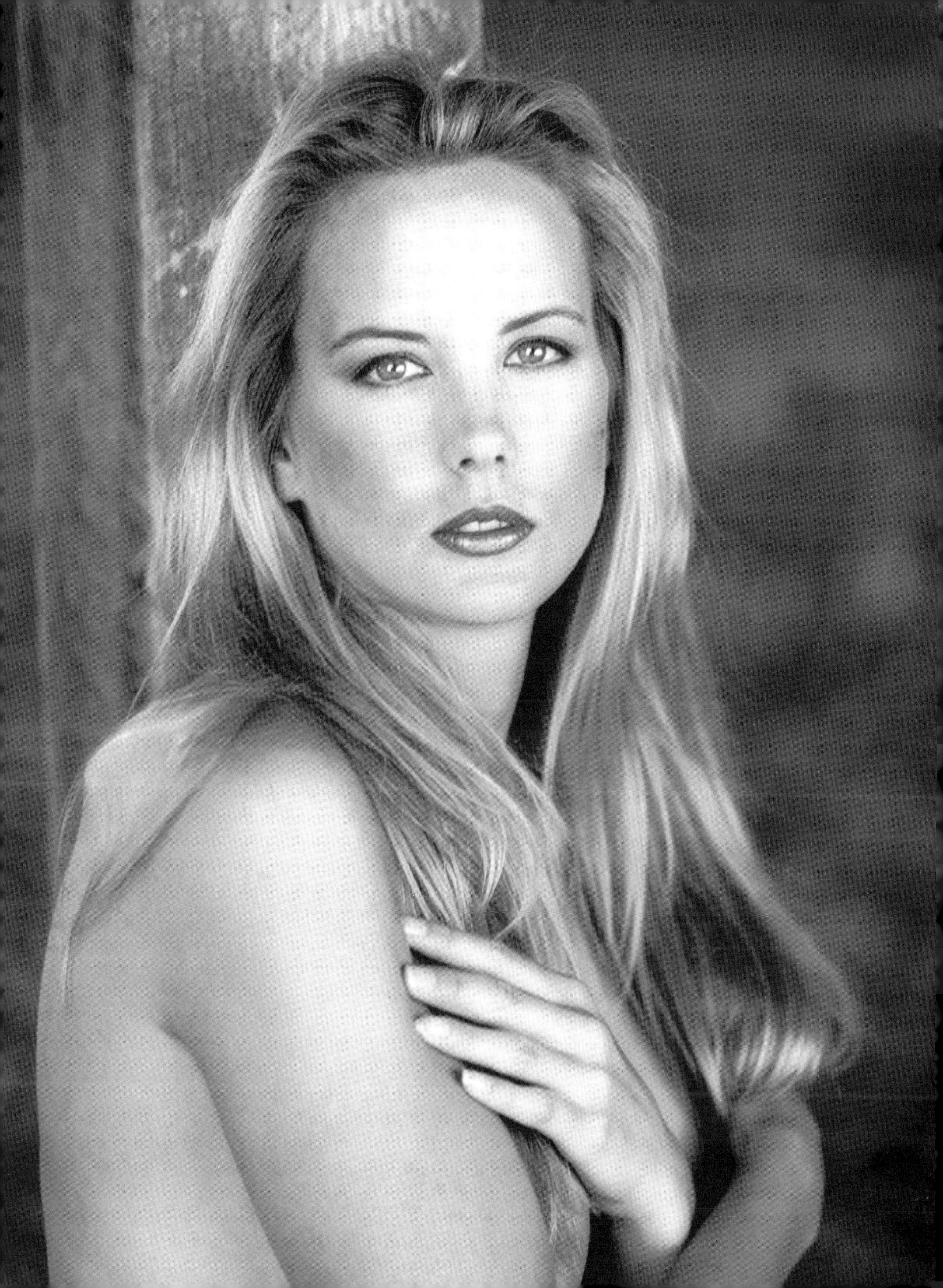

■ Background

The background is created using light. A strobe head placed behind the model and set two stops brighter than the light on her face ensures this pure white background.

■ Lighting

This image was created in the studio as I was trying out some different head shot lighting arrangements. A medium softbox was used to light the shadows on the model's face. This light creates the small square catch lights on the lower part of her eyes which make them seem to sparkle with life. An umbrella was placed over the camera to light the top of her face. This light can be just barely picked out in the upper part of the model's eyes. Equal power was used to each head.

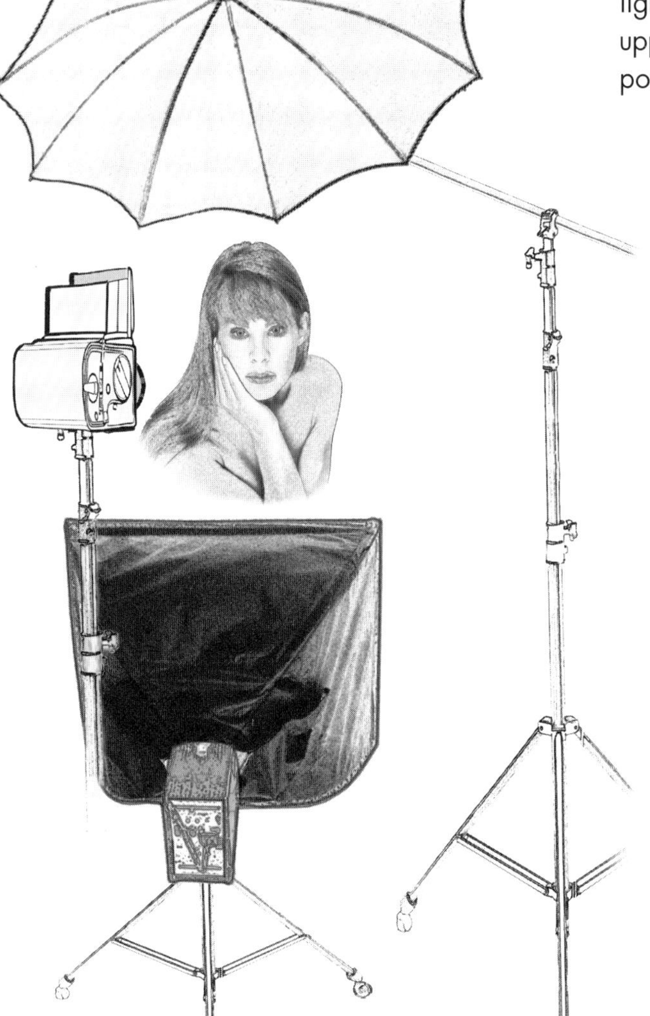

CAMERA
Hasselblad 503

LENS
150mm

FILM
Kodak TMX 100

LIGHTING
softbox, umbrella, two strobe heads

EQUIPMENT
tripod and cable release

MODEL
Annette McKnight

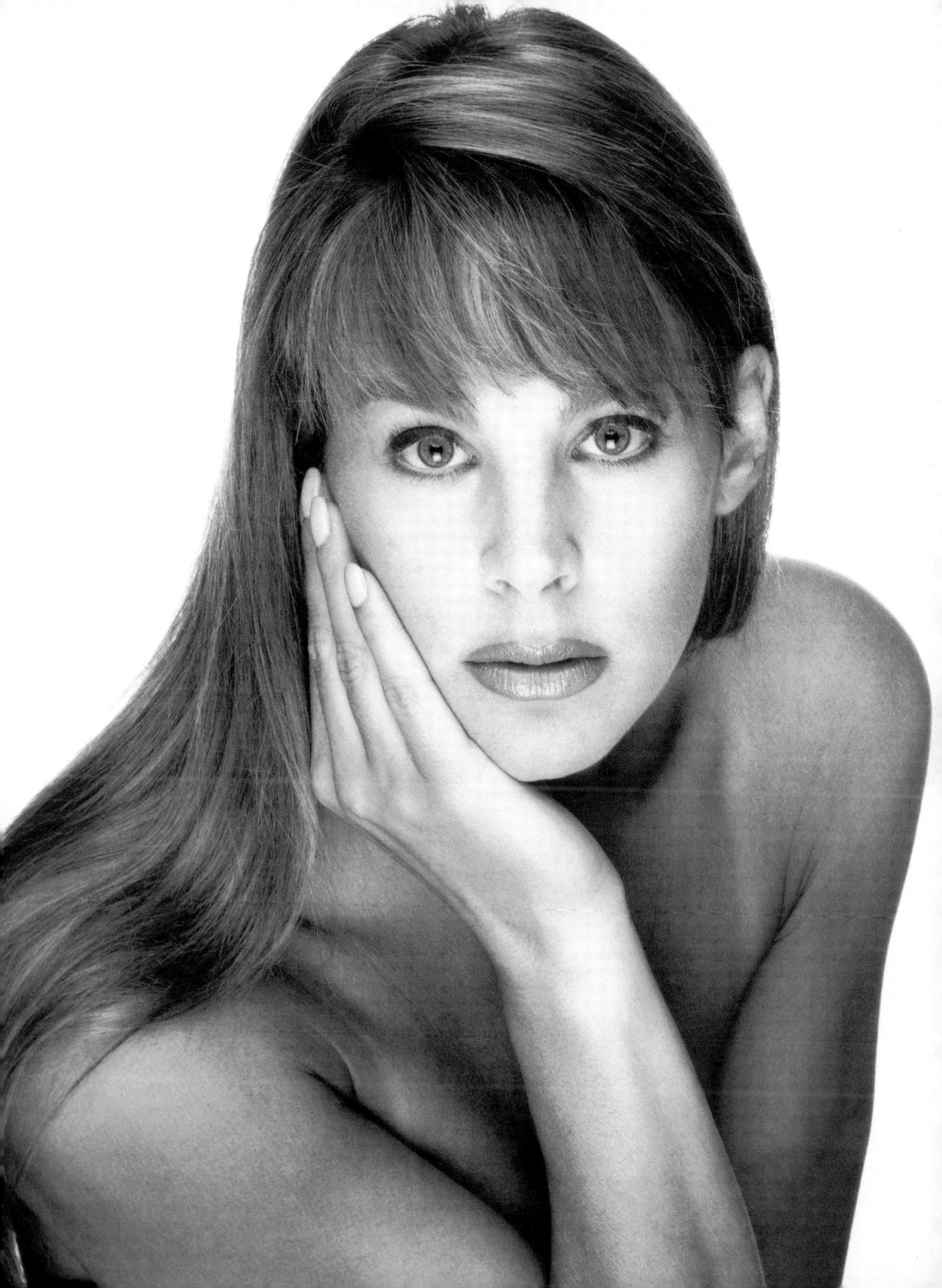

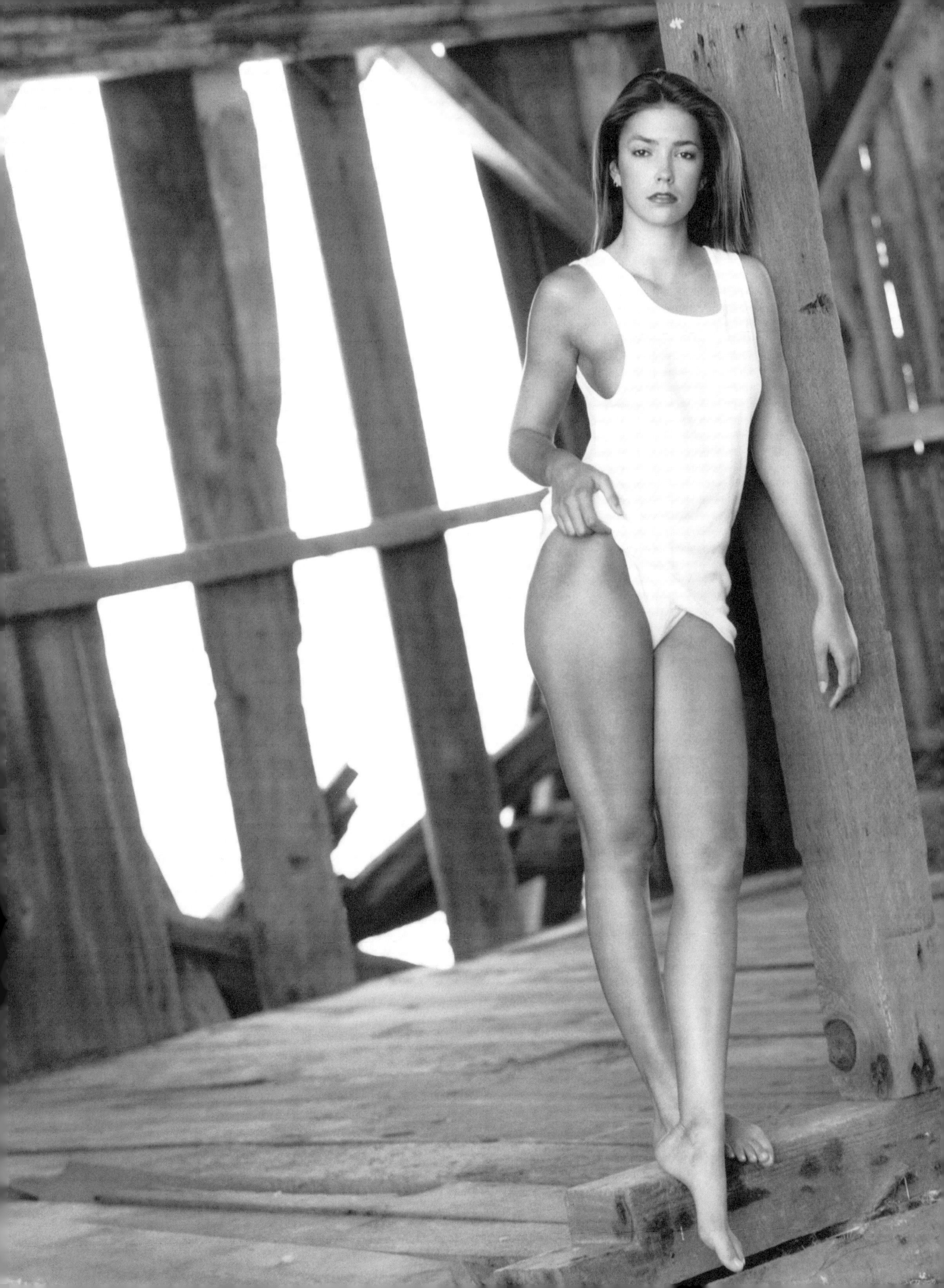

■ Posing

This is a great pose for a model with long, slim legs who doesn't want to pose nude. The high French cut of the underwear lengthens the visual line of the leg, and the wealth of vertical elements in the background increases the visual sense of length you get when looking at the photo.

■ Exposure

Exposing the photograph for the light inside (about *f* 5.6), rather than the bright light of the summer sky outside (about *f* 22), washes out the background completely, keeping the visual focus on the model. The choice of white clothing for the model helps to keep the bright white background from becoming overwhelming or distracting.

BILL LEMON'S HINTS AND TIPS:
When shooting on location, try to look at your setting with a creative eye. Even if you have previously decided on a series of poses, a good setting will often inspire you to envision new poses. Pay special attention to natural light phenomena (such as light beams through the boards of an old barn). These can often be used to your advantage!

CAMERA
Hasselblad 500CM
LENS
150mm
FILM
Kodak TMX 100
LIGHTING
natural
EQUIPMENT
tripod and cable release
MODEL
Kelly Wolfe

■ Posing

When going out in the field, it's a good idea to have a few poses and locations in mind. These should be images you think will make good use of the model's assets (a beautiful face, long legs, great eyes, etc.), and to produce the kind of images she is looking for (softly sensual, artistic nude, fashion, etc.). It is also a good idea to keep in mind the model's energy level and enthusiasm, as well as her level of experience in front of the camera. Having a point to start from can be very helpful in making the model feel comfortable and in developing a rapport with her. Once this is established, new ideas tend to evolve and you can progress from your original ideas and on to new ones.

This location in which this image was shot is one I had thought out in advance. The model is posed on the back of a large flatbed truck, and her body is framed by the smokestack to the right, and the tires to the lower left. The image is shot using natural light, but I had the model tip her head up to fill in the shadows under her lips and nose. The bent leg and uplifted arms add a sensual line to her body.

"The bent leg and uplifted arms add a sensual line to her body."

CAMERA
Pentax 6x7
LENS
200mm
FILM
Kodak Plus X 100
LIGHTING
natural
EQUIPMENT
tripod and cable release
MODEL
Brandi Clymer

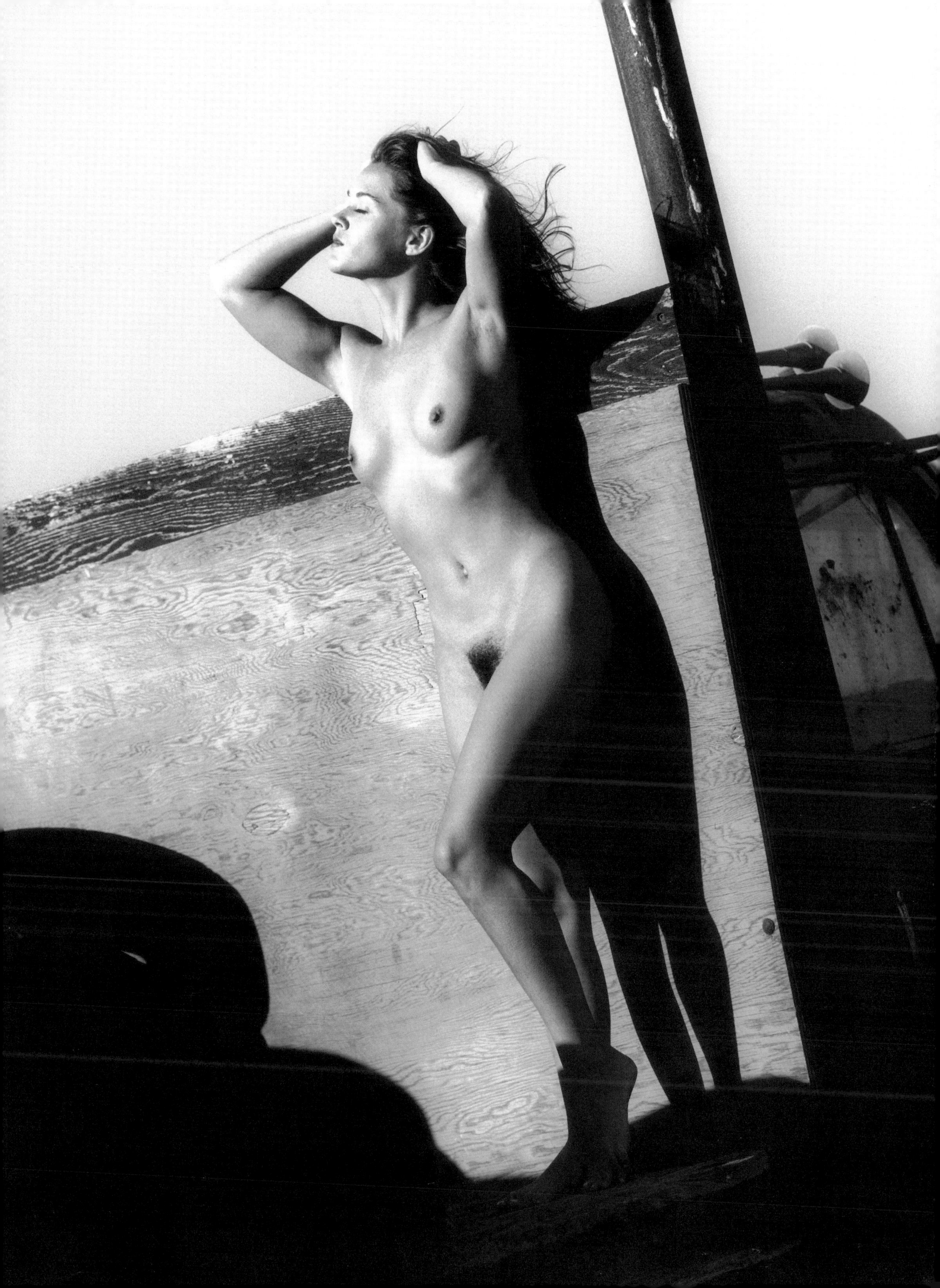

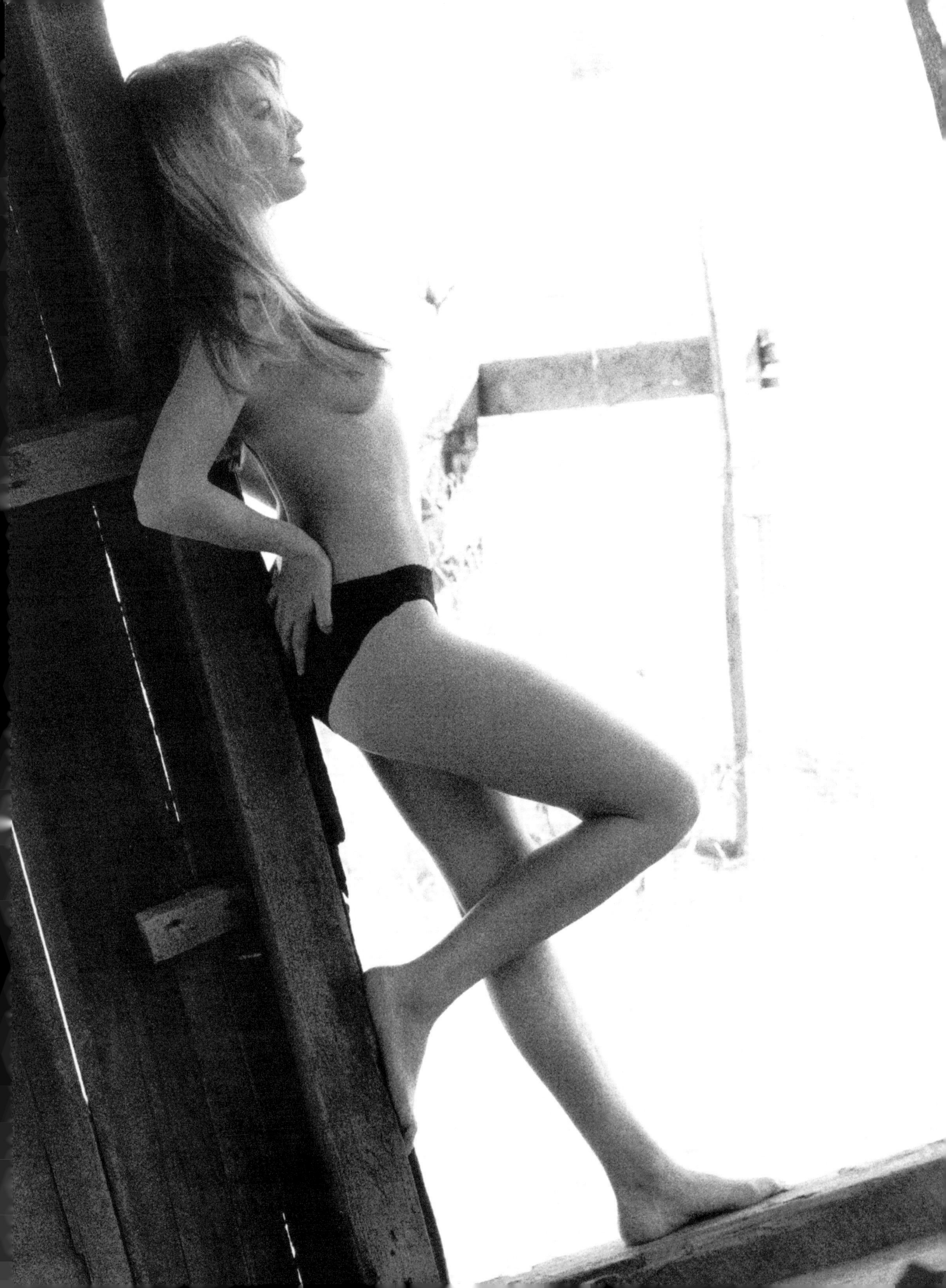

■ Exposure
A high shutter speed (as fast as 1/8000 sec.) with this film helps preserve the accurate skin tones in this image while letting the background become well overexposed.

■ Composition
This image was shot just inside the back door of the old barn. The softly illuminated silhouette shows off one of this model's strongest assets — her great legs. The model's hair was also arranged such that a few strands fell down over her breast. This adds a nice element of softness to the image.

■ Clothing
The choice of dark underwear separates the model more from the bright background than would white clothing, so it was a natural choice for this image.

CAMERA
Nikon 8008

LENS
80-200 mm

FILM
Kodak TMZ 3200 rated at 1600

LIGHTING
natural

EQUIPMENT
tripod

MODEL
Laureen Barnes

■ Lighting

This photograph was taken using a large (4′x8′) moveable door and window prop which I had in my studio. The only source of illumination is a large (4′x6′) softbox placed on the opposite side of the window from the model. The light from this is further diffused by the sheer window curtains.

■ Composition

This is a flattering and sensual image for a model who does not wish to work nude or semi-nude. Note that the largely low-key effect here is probably best suited to a model with dark hair. It is a soft and extremely feminine pose.

■ Printing

The addition of a black border at the edge of the photograph keeps the white curtains sharply defined within the frame and helps balance the dark areas at the right of the photograph.

"It is a soft and extremely feminine pose."

CAMERA
Nikon F3

LENS
85mm

FILM
Kodak TMZ 3200 rated at 1600

LIGHTING
large softbox

MODEL
Kerry Rodriguez

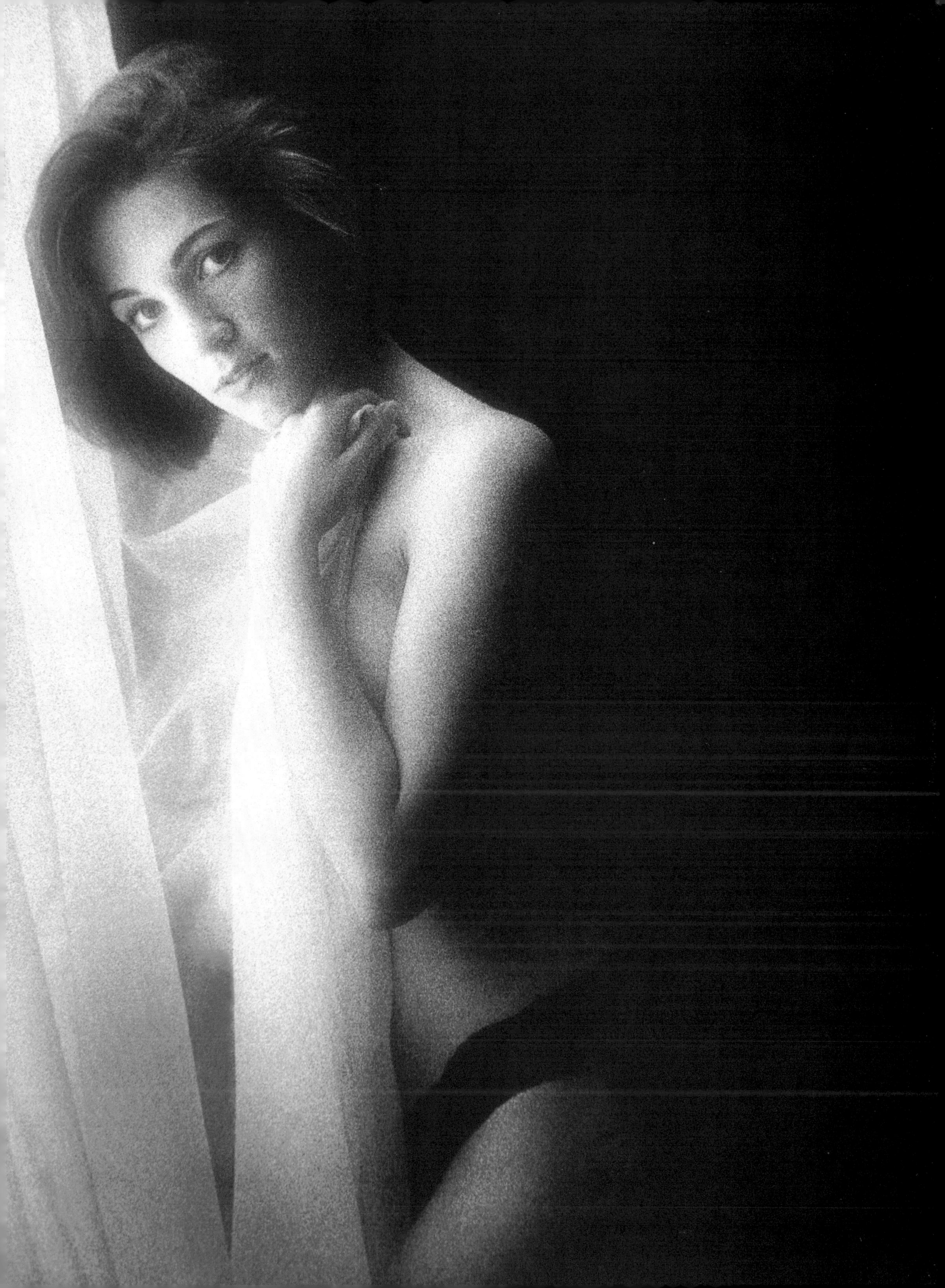

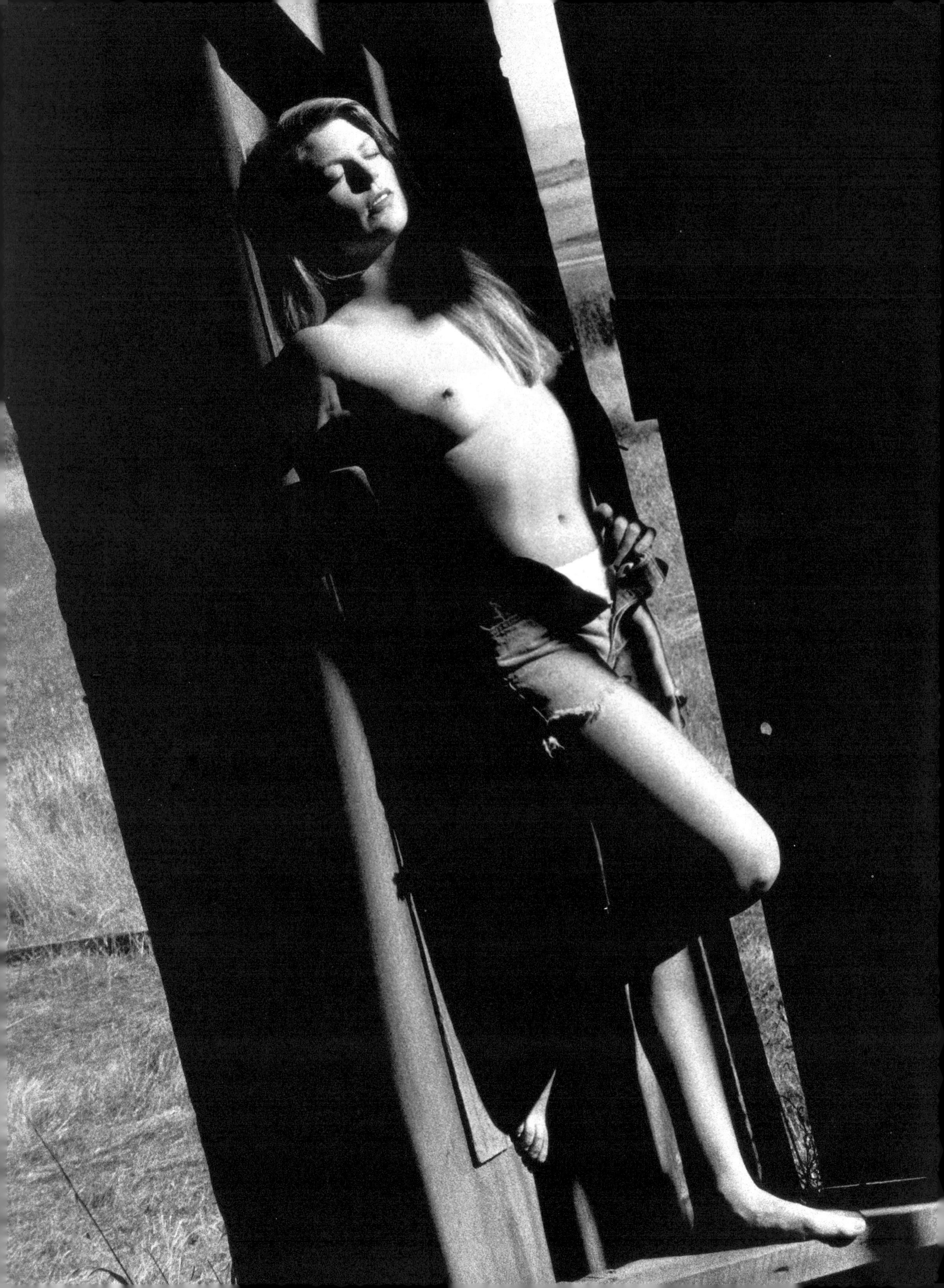

■ Clothing

In many of the images in this book you will notice that the models have open zippers or unbuttoned shirts. This choice isn't made to create a sense of voyeurism, but really has an important role in making the image look a little softer. Imagine this photo taken with the zipper up. It would change the entire tone of the image. In the same way, shooting this photograph with shorts undone but no underwear would also change the tone of the image dramatically. When making clothing choices, it's important to be aware that small changes can often send big signals to the viewer of the image.

■ Setting up the Shot

For this photograph, the light reading was take off the model's face, since this was the most important part of the image to me. The camera was also slightly tilted to add dimension to the image. Notice also the landscape visible through the boards behind the model; this suggests a greater sense of the setting to the viewer.

"...small changes can often send big signals to the viewer..."

CAMERA
Nikon 8008

LENS
80-200mm

FILM
Kodak TMZ 3200 rated at 1600

LIGHTING
natural

EQUIPMENT
tripod

MODEL
Laureen Barnes

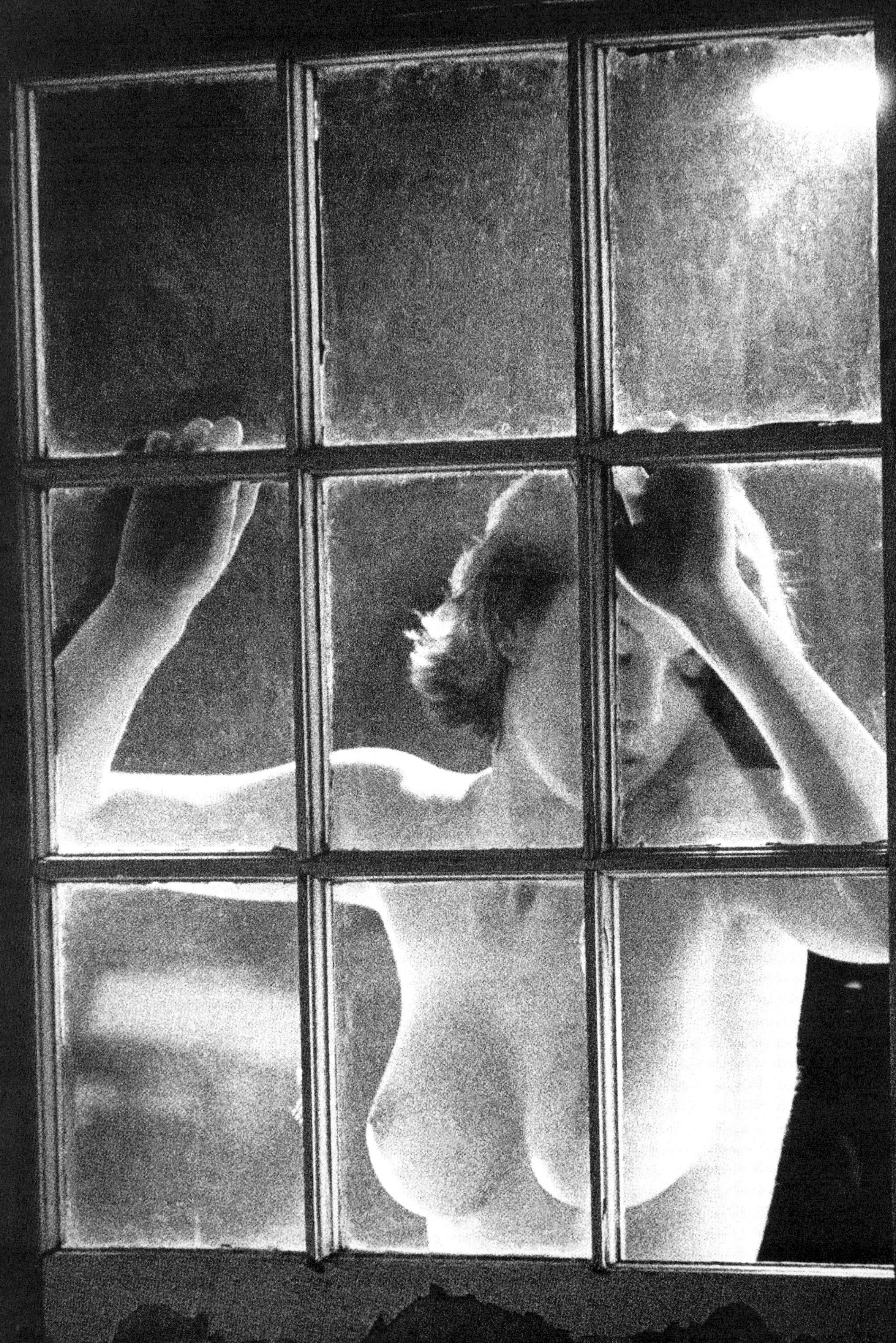

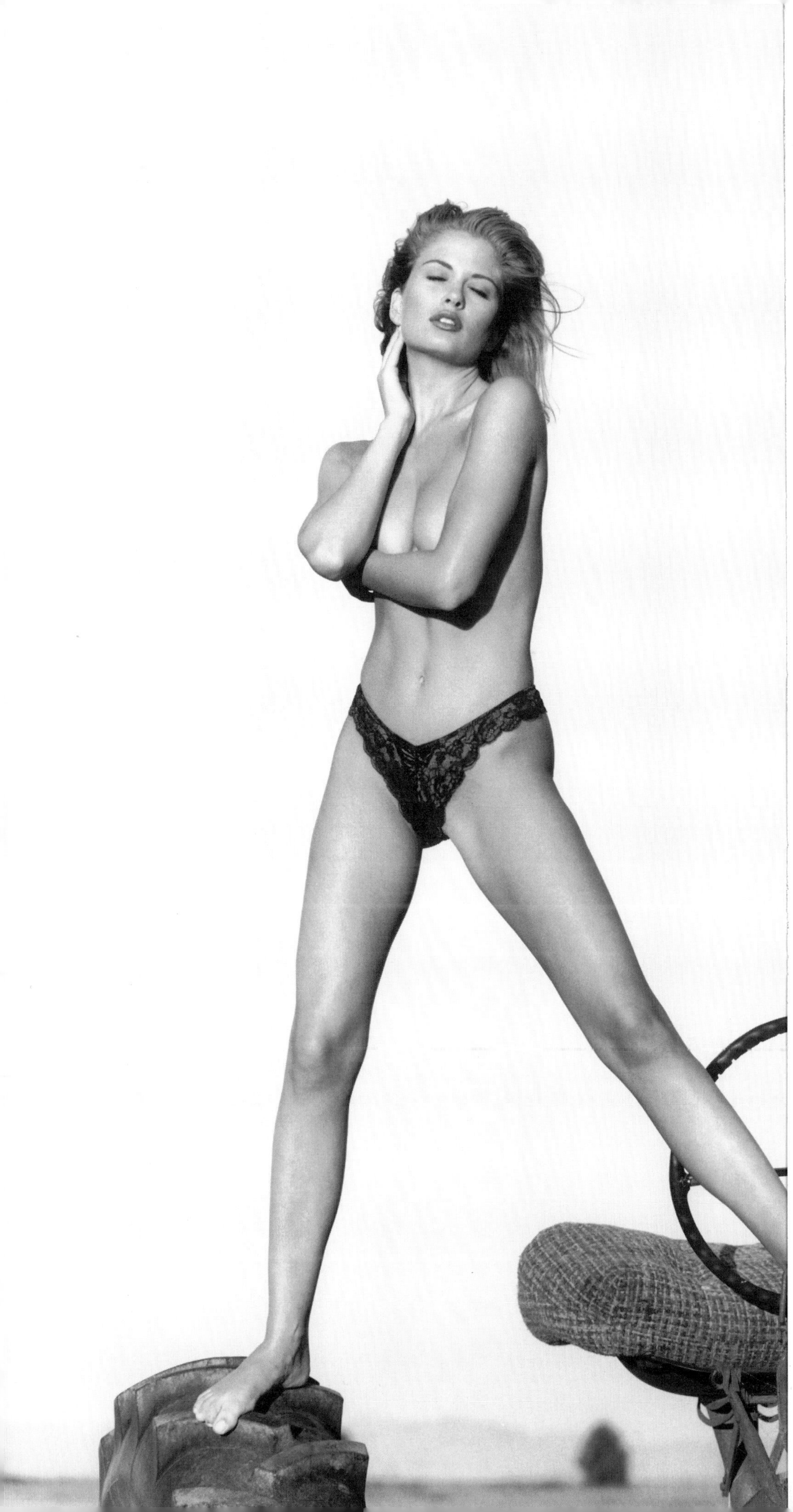

■ Lighting

An overhead light was used and is visible in the upper right-hand corner of the image. An additional silver reflector was placed in front of the model to illuminate the front of her body. It must be placed on the same side of the glass to eliminate possible reflections.

■ Posing

When using an element like this window in an image, it is especially important to be conscious of how the body is broken up in the image. Areas to be especially careful about are the eyes and neck.

■ Setting

This image was created in my studio at a window which makes up part of a dividing wall constructed of old barn wood.

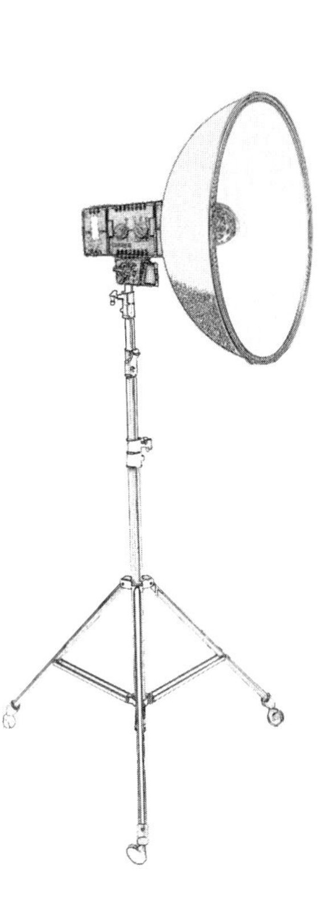

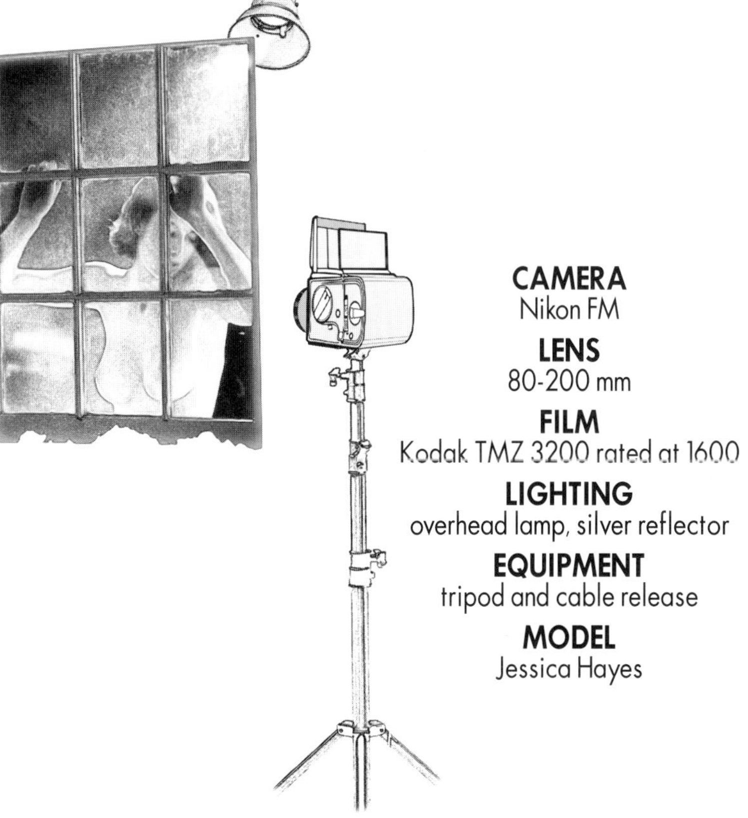

CAMERA
Nikon FM

LENS
80-200 mm

FILM
Kodak TMZ 3200 rated at 1600

LIGHTING
overhead lamp, silver reflector

EQUIPMENT
tripod and cable release

MODEL
Jessica Hayes

■ Exposure

This photograph was taken with the setting sun at my back. I shot in this light at about *f*16 in order to catch the detail on the equipment and on the model's body. The far away background is allowed to go completely soft.

■ Posing

A dramatic pose like this is both eye-catching and flattering to a model with a great body. It especially draws attention to the model's long legs. Dark underwear was chosen to help the model stand out sharply against the very light background.

■ Setting

Although very little of the
equipment upon which the
left within the frame, the s
makes a little go a long w
ingly small elements like t
huge visual impact when
taken as a whole.

"It especially draws attention to the model's long legs."

CAMERA
Hasselblad 5

LENS
150mm

FILM
Kodak TMX

LIGHTIN
natural

EQUIPME
tripod and cable

MODEL
Dale Colm

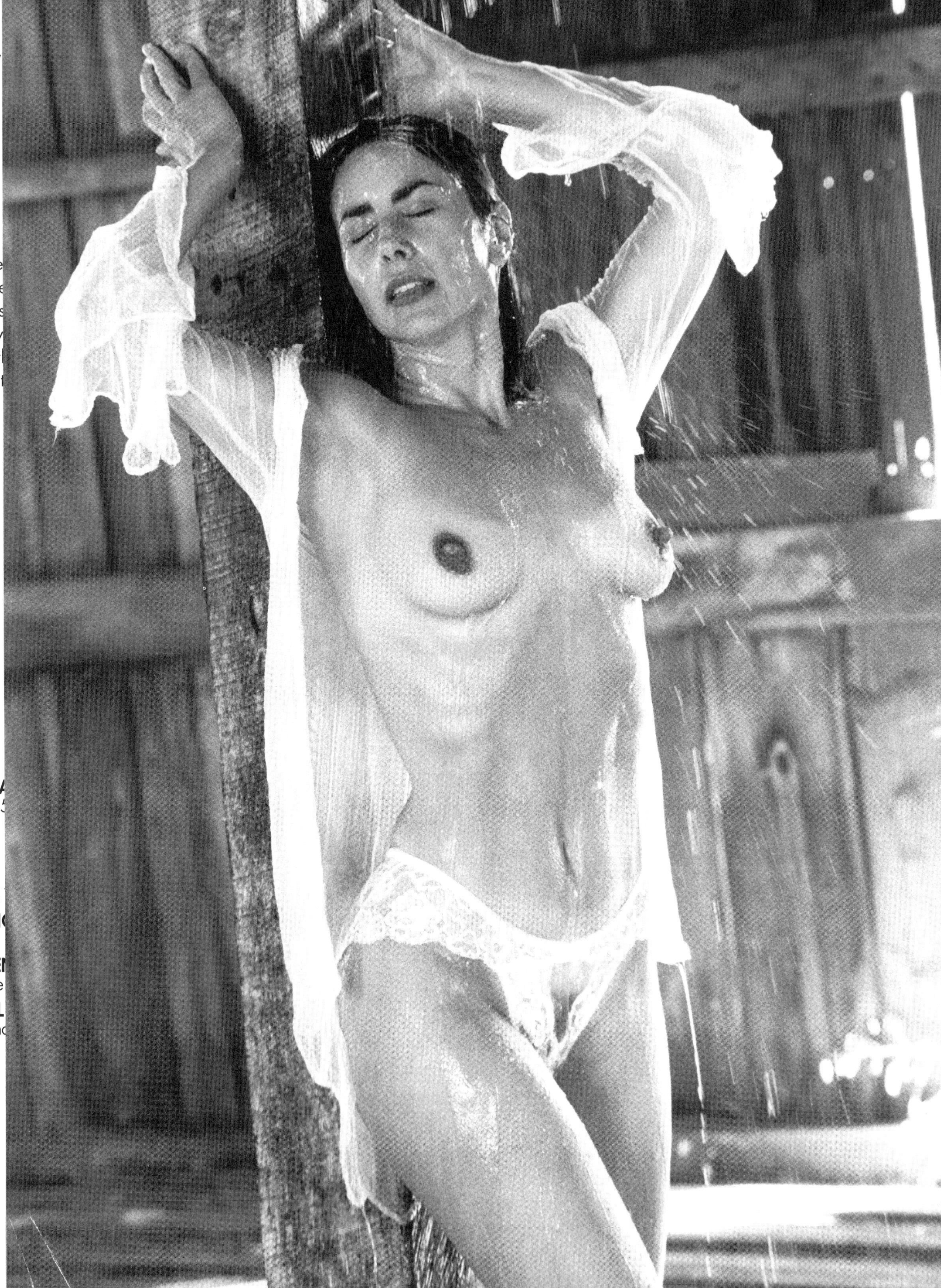

■ Water

Water can add a sensual dimension to an image, but it can also present certain challenges. For instance, the model can become uncomfortable and cold. Also, unless water shots are your only images of the session, they will either have to be shot last, or models will need time to fix their hair and make-up and dry off before moving to the next setting. Finally, if using a portable water source such as the one used in this image, you will have to shoot fast, since the water will only last for a short time.

■ Posing

The model started this shoot with her blouse buttoned, and this would have made a nice image too. As we shot, she undid her blouse, and this makes the image even better, as I was able to capture the rivulets of water running over her bare chest. Lifting the arms makes breasts look their best.

"Water can add a sensual dimension to an image..."

CAMERA
Nikon 8008

LENS
80-200 mm

FILM
Kodak TMZ 3200 rated at 1600

LIGHTING
natural

MODEL
Tina Marturana

■ Lighting

This head shot was taken in my studio with a very simple lighting arrangement consisting of two Norman heads. One was placed on top of the other. This image contains a great deal of contrast and a full range of tones from black to white which give it high visual impact. The light primarily highlights her face and arms, but also adds depth to the image by falling softly on her upper chest.

■ Pose

This pose, which brings more than the model's face into the image, is nicely framed by the model's arms and hands. The hand lifted to her hair is a very feminine gesture that fits the soft femininity of the image. To achieve this image, the model was posed on a rollable platform in the studio, and sat with her elbows on her knees.

"The hand lifted to her hair is a very feminine gesture..."

CAMERA
Hasselblad 503
LENS
150mm
FILM
Agfapan 25
LIGHTING
two Norman heads
EQUIPMENT
tripod and cable release
MODEL
Karryn Eisele

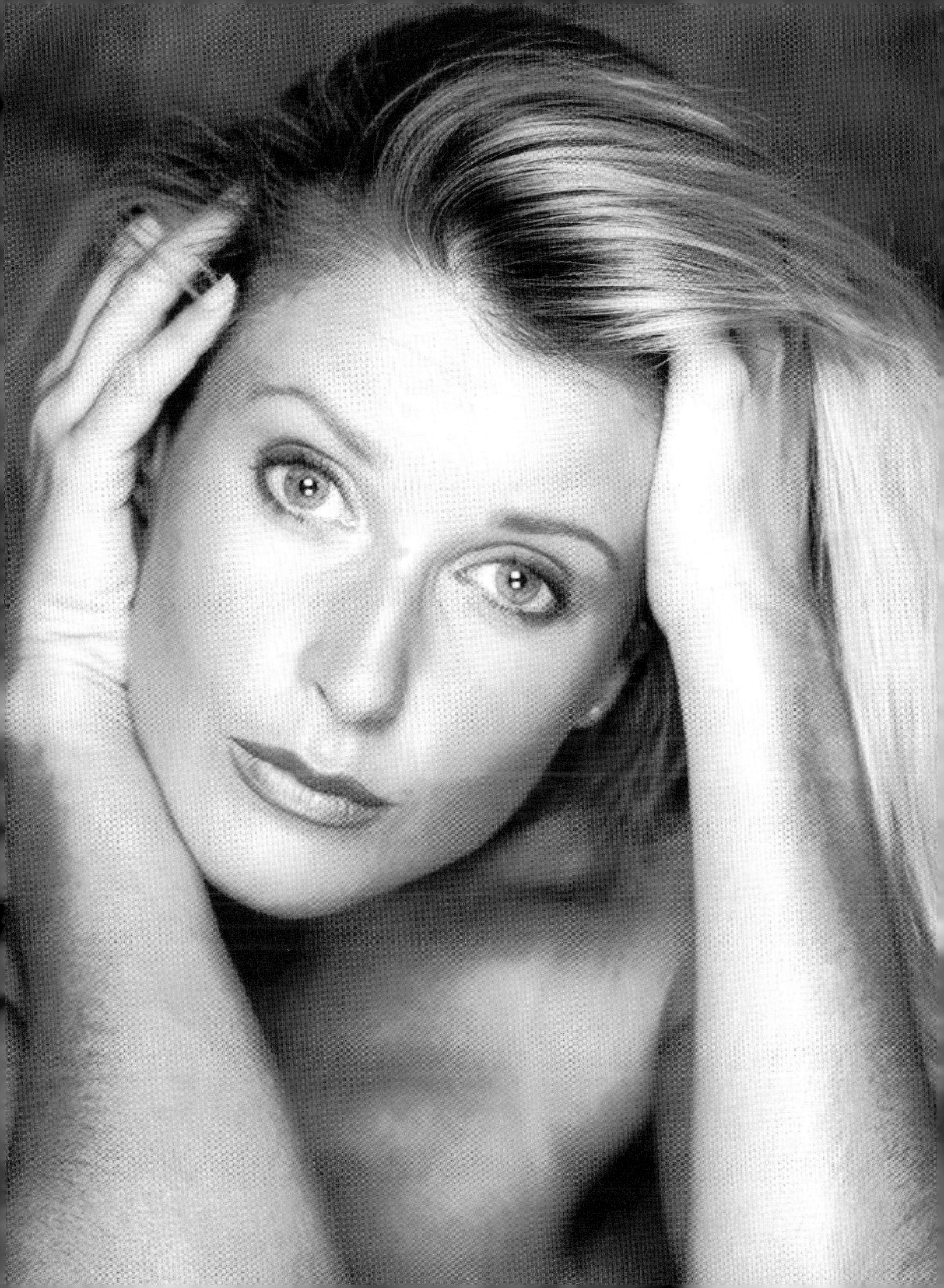

■ Lighting

This photograph was created using only available light. Technically, careful attention is paid to detail. The model is posed in order to take maximum advantage of the light and create the highlights in her hair and rim lighting on her left thigh. These lighting effects serve to separate her from the dark background, and are, again, achieved simply by making effective use of available light.

■ Water

When I plan to shoot with water, I create a shower effect on location by using a five gallon bucket with holes in the bottom. The holes are plugged with a stopper attached to a string, and when I am set to shoot, I have the model pull the string to start the flow of water. Using a high speed film serves to freeze the water in the image.

"The model is posed in order to take maximum advantage of the light..."

CAMERA
Nikon 8008

LENS
80-200mm

FILM
Kodak TMZ 3200 rated at 1600

LIGHTING
natural

EQUIPMENT
tripod

MODEL
Kerry Rodriguez

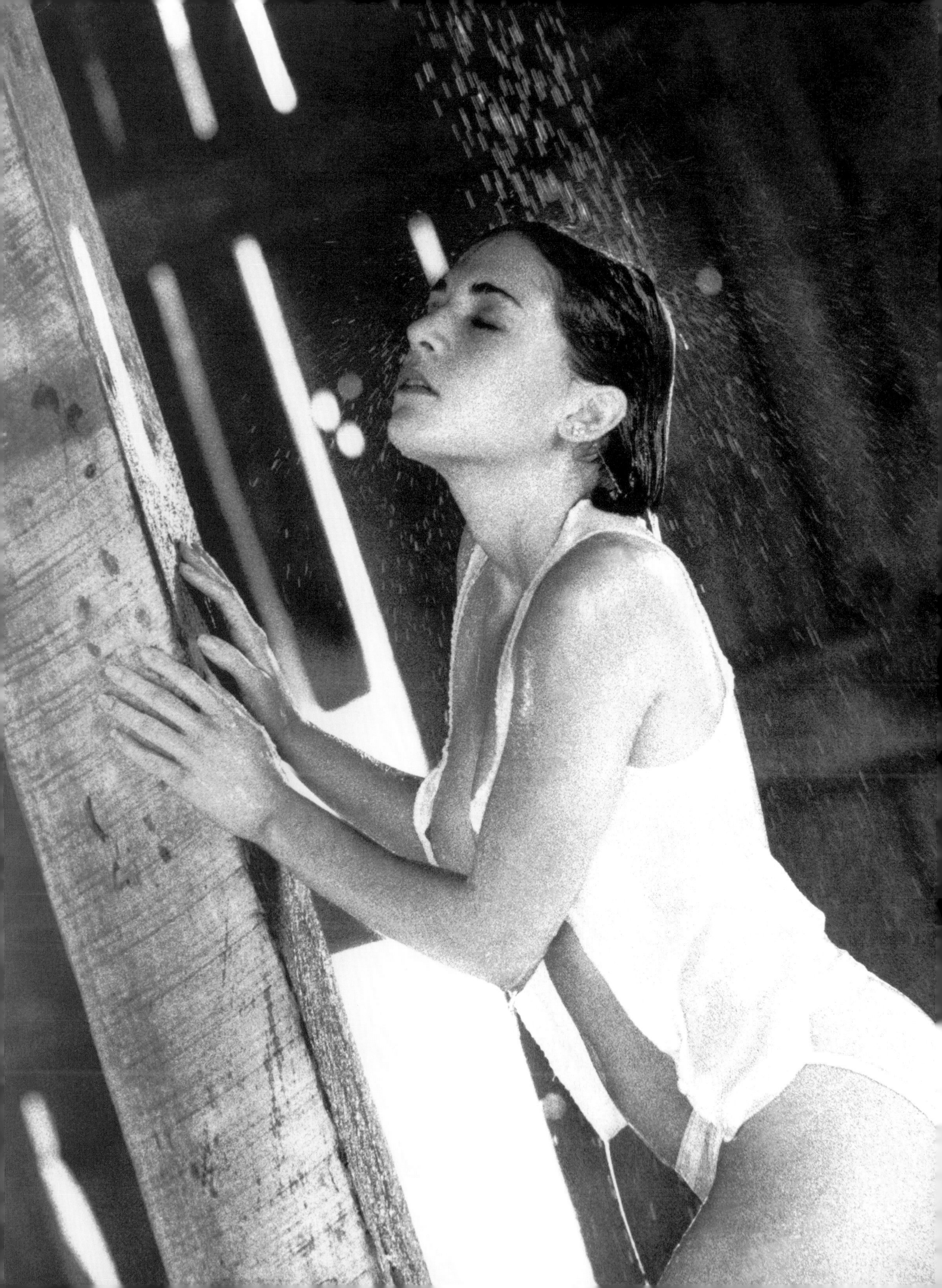

■ Setting

This photograph was created in my studio with a background of black velvet spread out on a platform. As you can see, it makes the model almost seem to float in the frame, and emphasizes her beautiful, smooth skin.

■ Composition

The model's arms (especially her left one which bends across most of the bottom of the image) frame her face against the dark background. The dark teddy is revealing, but still allows her body to blend off into the darkness at the left of the image. The one exposed earring adds a small, glittering area of high contrast at the center of the photograph.

■ Setting up the shot

Kodak Panatomic X, in my opinion, is one of the best black and white films ever made. Unfortunately, it is no longer available. To create this image, the camera was mounted high above the model on a ladder, using a Superclamp with an attached tripod head.

"...it makes the model almost seem to float in the frame..."

CAMERA
Hasselblad 503

LENS
150mm

FILM
Kodak Panatomic X32

LIGHTING
extra-large softbox

EQUIPMENT
Superclamp with tripod head, ladder

MODEL
Kirsten Harrison

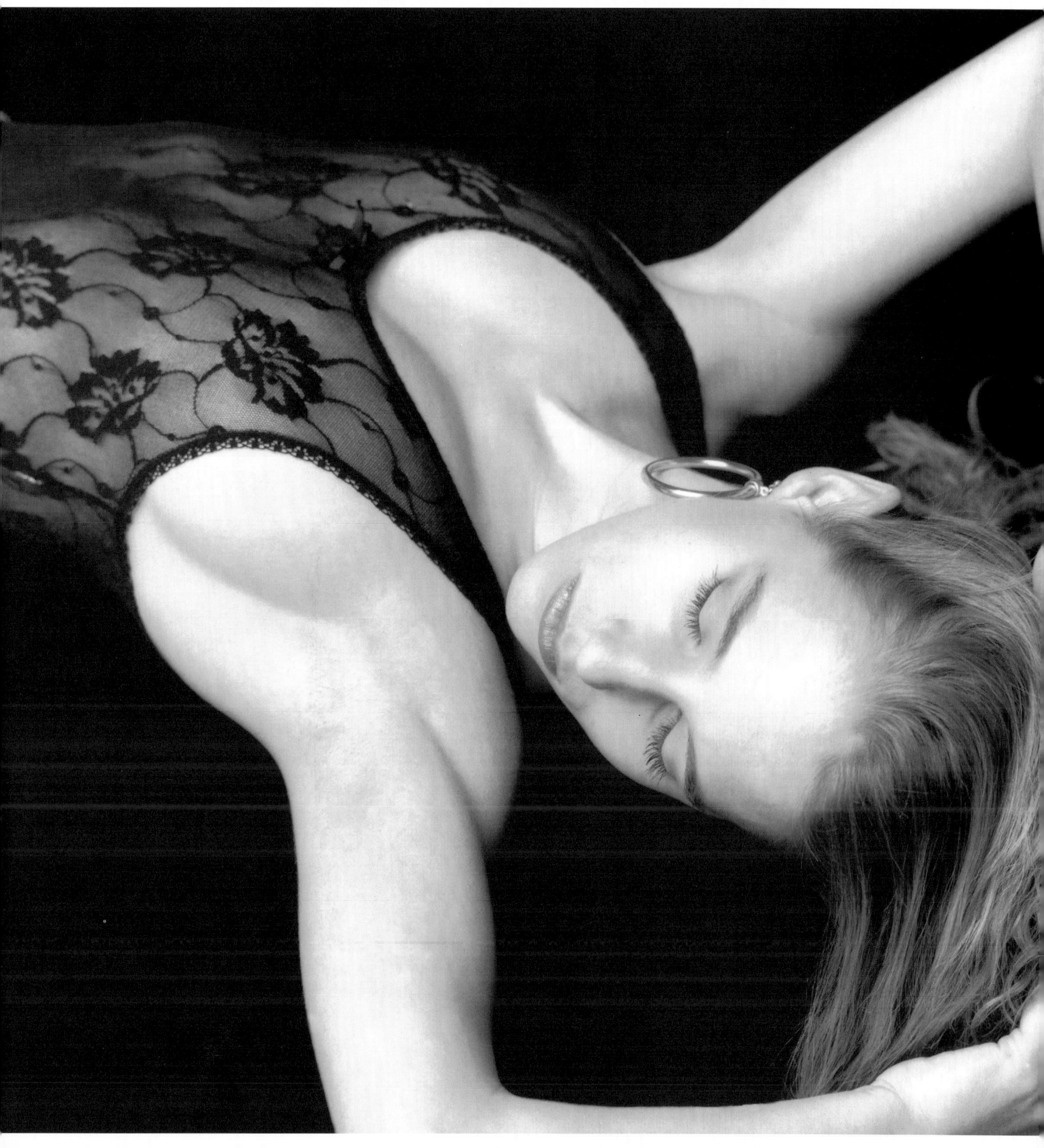

■ Mood

I wanted the light in this image to convey a sense of solitude and tranquility. The northern light just inside the door of the barn was perfect for capturing this emotion. The model's gaze, cast down and away from the camera, as well as her relaxed pose, help emphasize the emotion.

■ Tilt

The camera was slightly tilted to create this photograph. Notice how the model still seems to be reclining, but not as though she is about to tip over. Moderation is the key to making this camera trick work effectively.

BILL LEMON'S HINTS AND TIPS:
When you have a particular image in mind, you may have to photograph two or three different models to achieve it. Not every model works for every image. Don't give up if the first attempt in creating an image doesn't meet your expectations.

CAMERA
Nikon 8008

LENS
80-200mm

FILM
Kodak TMZ 3200 rated at 1600

LIGHTING
natural

EQUIPMENT
tripod

MODEL
Racine Mason

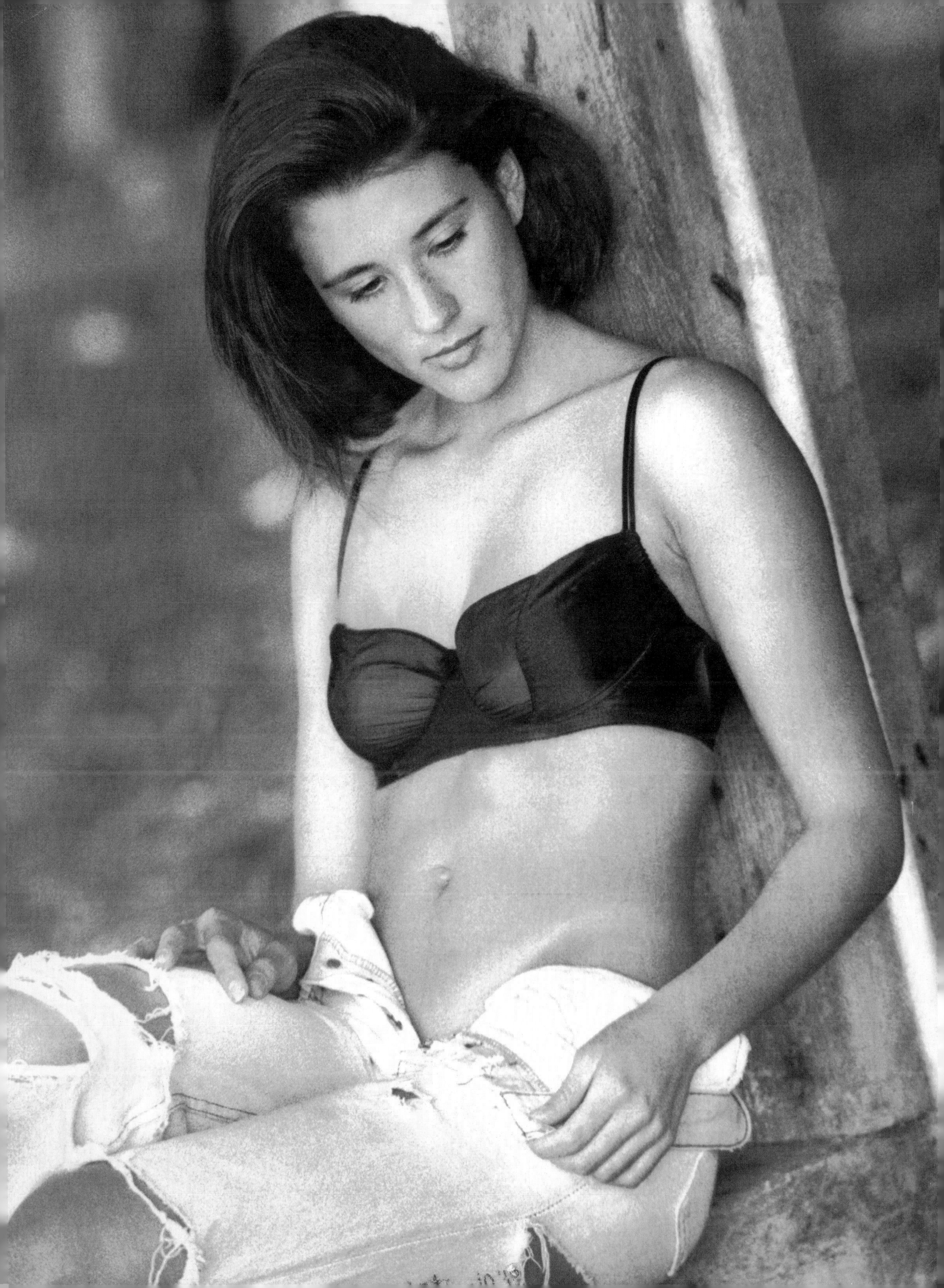

■ Photographer's Comments
This image is one adapted from the work of Italian photographer Marco Glaviano. With his image in mind, I decided to try to create this one to see if I could achieve the same visual impact.

■ Makeup
I used an assistant for this shot, since the model had to be carefully prepared to achieve this image. My assistant misted the model with water and placed sand on her body almost grain by grain. She also worked with the model's hair to give it this wet and sultry look. This model wears make-up that is much more dramatic than the models in most of the images in this book.

■ Lighting
A main light (at 400 watt second) was placed over the camera to provide the majority of the image's illumination. A polished aluminum reflector was positioned below the model to help illuminate the shadows on her face.

"...the model had to be carefully prepared to achieve this image."

CAMERA
Hasselblad 503
LENS
150mm
FILM
Agfa Pan 25
LIGHTING
natural
EQUIPMENT
tripod
MODEL
Antoinette Da Silva

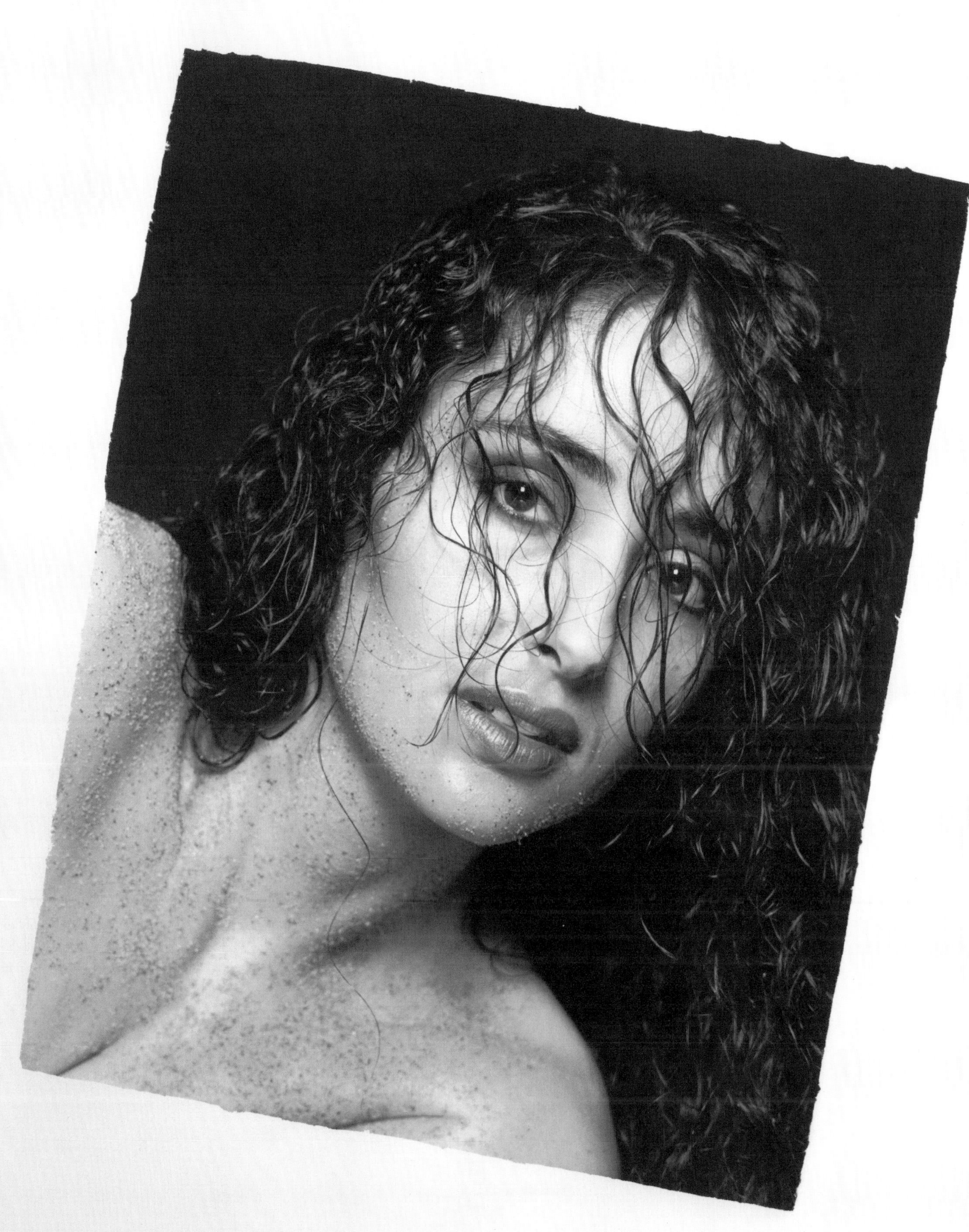

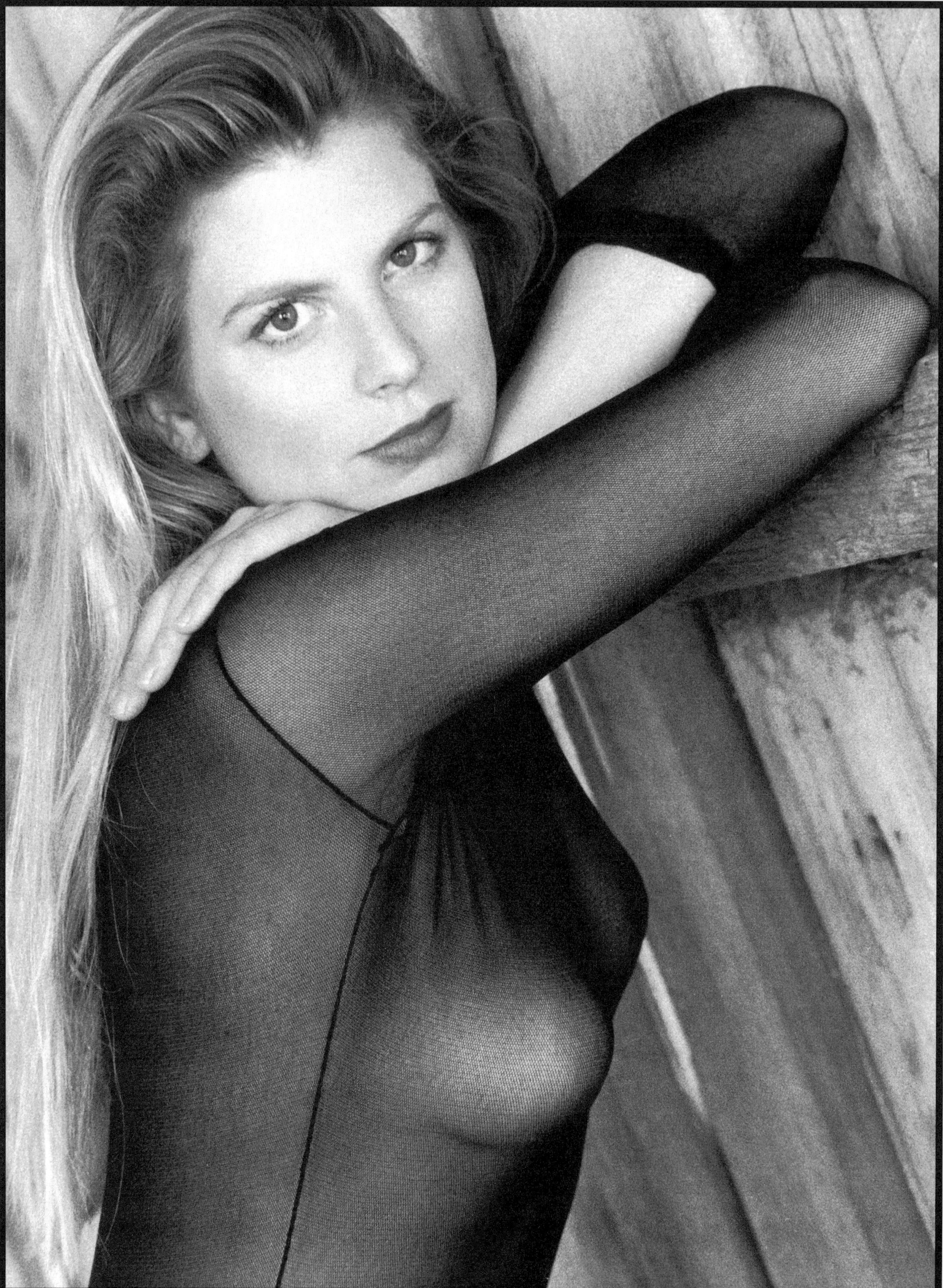

■ Clothing

This sheer, long sleeved, black teddy is a garment that I use frequently. It provides a nice medium between exposure and concealment, and always looks sophisticated and classic.

Here, the garment's dark color works with the relatively low key tonalities of the image, and helps to make the model's face the focal point of the photograph. Imagine this photograph shot with the model wearing white. Immediately, some of the impact of this image would be lost because your eye would not be drawn so instantly to the model's face.

■ Lighting

The soft northern natural lighting in this image is a perfect complement for the model's soft face and her facial expression. The relaxed pose also complements the lighting tones and overall mood of the photograph.

"...the garment's dark color adds to the overall low key tonalities of the image..."

CAMERA
Nikon 8008

LENS
80-200mm

FILM
Kodak TMZ 3200 rated at 1600

LIGHTING
natural

MODEL
Laureen Barnes

■ Posing

Some models simply do not feel comfortable working nude or even semi-nude. Still, this does not mean that you cannot create sensual and dramatic images. This model's gorgeous hair, face and body are the focus of this photograph. The soft lingerie top, and the high cut of her shorts makes the image very sensual without being revealing. Even her legs are not revealed, but rather hinted at by the very small area of her thigh which shows in the bottom right corner of the photograph.

The model is posed to show off her curvaceous body. The pose is made all the more dramatic by the contrast of these curves with the very straight lines of the post on which she is leaning.

■ Finishing Touches

Although they are understated, a few important elements contribute directly to the impact of this image. First, the tilt of the camera softens the image and positions the model's body beautifully in the frame. Second, the wind that catches the model's hair adds a great sense of movement and atmosphere. Lastly, a border added in printing contributes the final touch by attractively framing the image

CAMERA
Nikon 8008

LENS
80-200mm

FILM
Kodak TMZ 3200 rated at 1600

LIGHTING
natural

EQUIPMENT
tripod

MODEL
Jennifer Renner

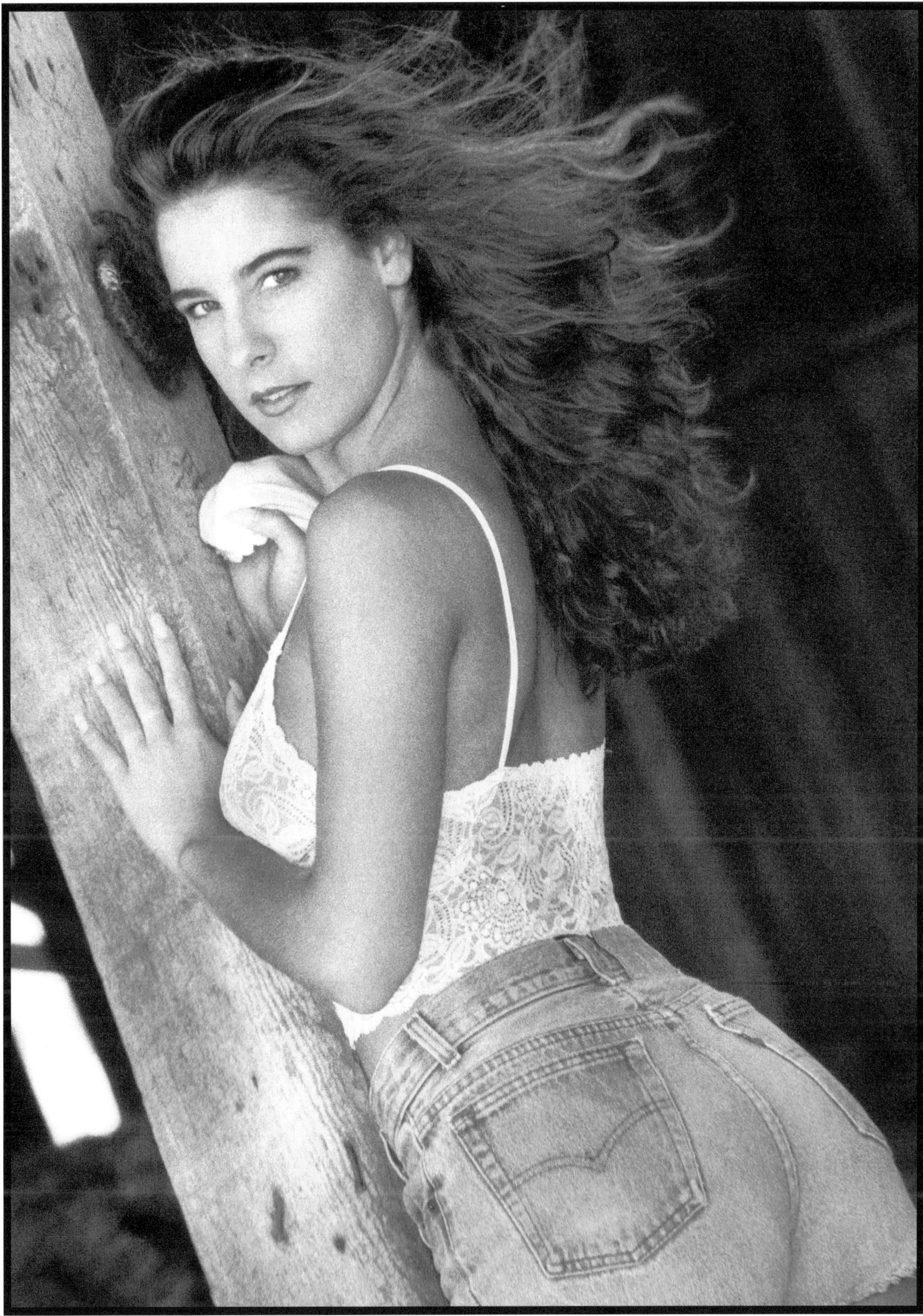

■ Setting

Mt. Tamalpias, a San Francisco Bay area landmark, is a majestic setting. It is also a photographic challenge. This image had to be taken at a certain time on a day that was extremely clear, with little wind. I was in the area shooting with this model when I realized the conditions were perfect.

■ Nail Polish

If I could change one thing about this images it would be the model's nail polish; I find it at odds with the rest of the image. When taking a spur of the moment opportunity, you often have to make concessions. In general, I prefer that model's don't wear dramatically colored polishes. I recommend clear polish, or a French manicure for nails that look groomed, but understated.

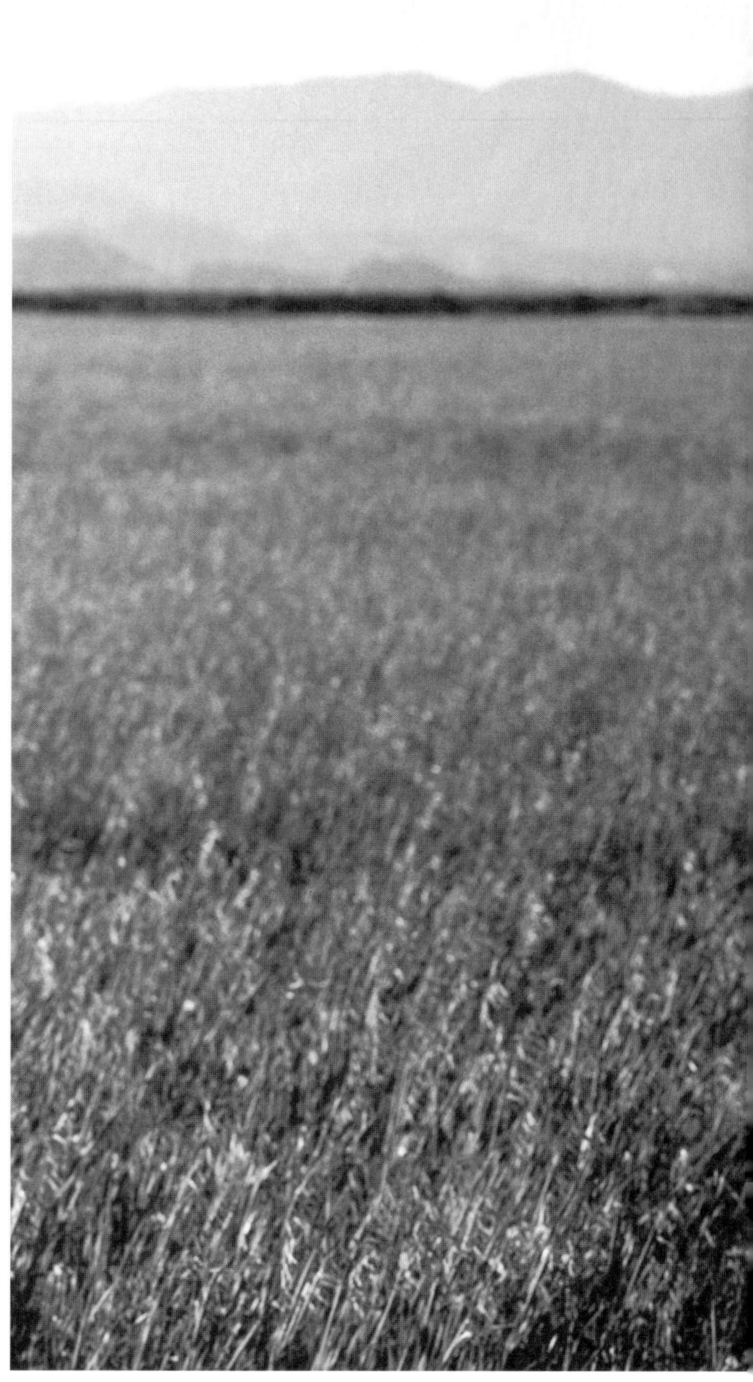

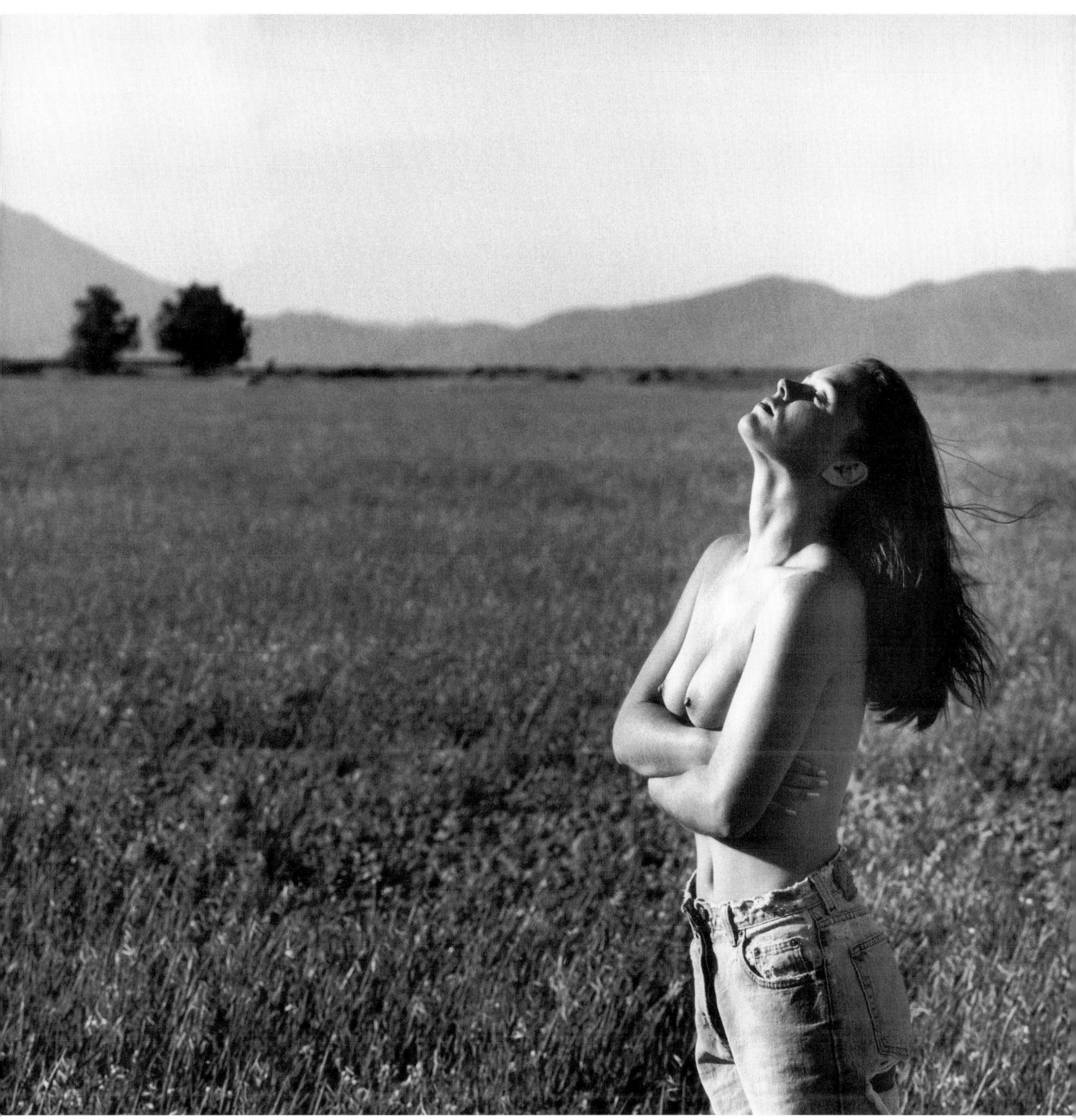

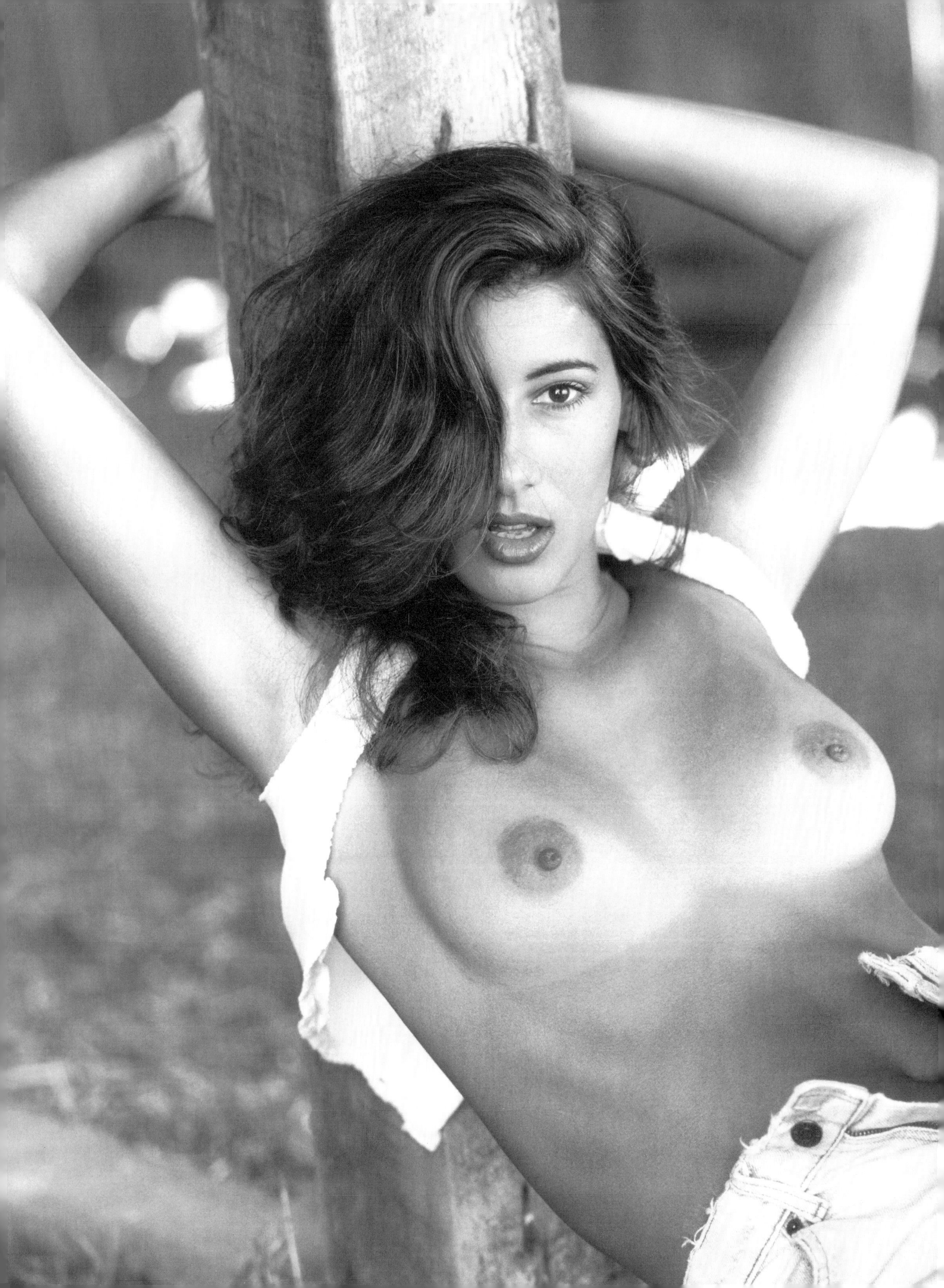

■ Models

Model's comfort levels will vary dramatically from individual to individual — and may even vary from one shoot to the next. I find that, generally, models become more and more comfortable with their bodies as they get older. Other factors, such as their relationship with their family or with a husband/boyfriend can also affect the kind of images a model may want to create.

The women in this book range in age from sixteen to forty-one, with the majority being between nineteen and twenty-three. Many of the women have children. Some are professional models, and some are not but were recommended to me by other clients. Yet others saw my work and wanted pictures of themselves.

In any case, it is important to pay attention to your models and what they feel comfortable doing.

Make sure also to tailor the poses and lighting you choose to each individual. As a shoot progresses, you should talk to the model and ask if she's comfortable. If not, it's time to rethink your strategies for the shoot. Remember, discomfort on the model's part is almost always obvious in the final product, and doesn't reflect well on you.

Encourage a model to recommend you to others. One of the nicest things I can hear from a model (besides how much she likes her pictures!) is that the shoot was fun and that she felt completely at ease.

CAMERA
Hasselblad 503
LENS
150 mm
FILM
Agfapan 100
LIGHTING
natural
MODEL
Lalanya Hudspeth

■ Photographer's Comments

All photographers like to get feedback on their work. With this image I had an unusual opportunity to see my photograph through a viewer's eye when a friend of mine drew an image based on this photo. I've had a few of my photos drawn, and would recommend the experience to others. It's a very interesting way to get a new perspective on your photography.

■ Tan lines

While it might be tempting to cover up tan lines, its really a matter of person preference. I don't find that I mind them, as long as they are even. Here, the tans lines on this model's breasts actually work well in the overall image by accentuating her bare chest.

"I had an unusual opportunity to see my photograph through a viewer's eye..."

CAMERA
Hasselblad 503
LENS
150mm
FILM
Agfapan 100
LIGHTING
natural
EQUIPMENT
tripod and cable release
MODEL
Laylana Hudspeth

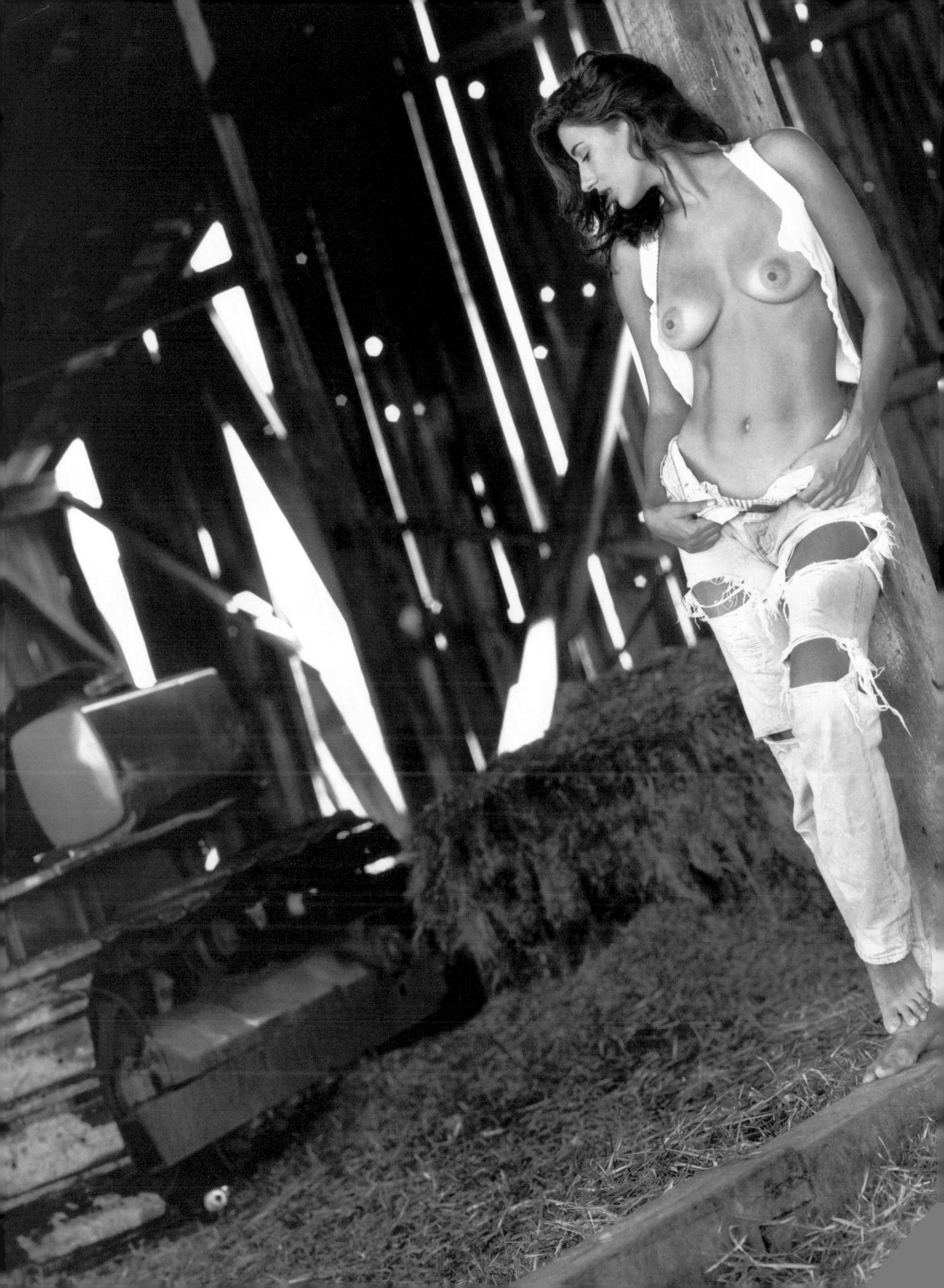

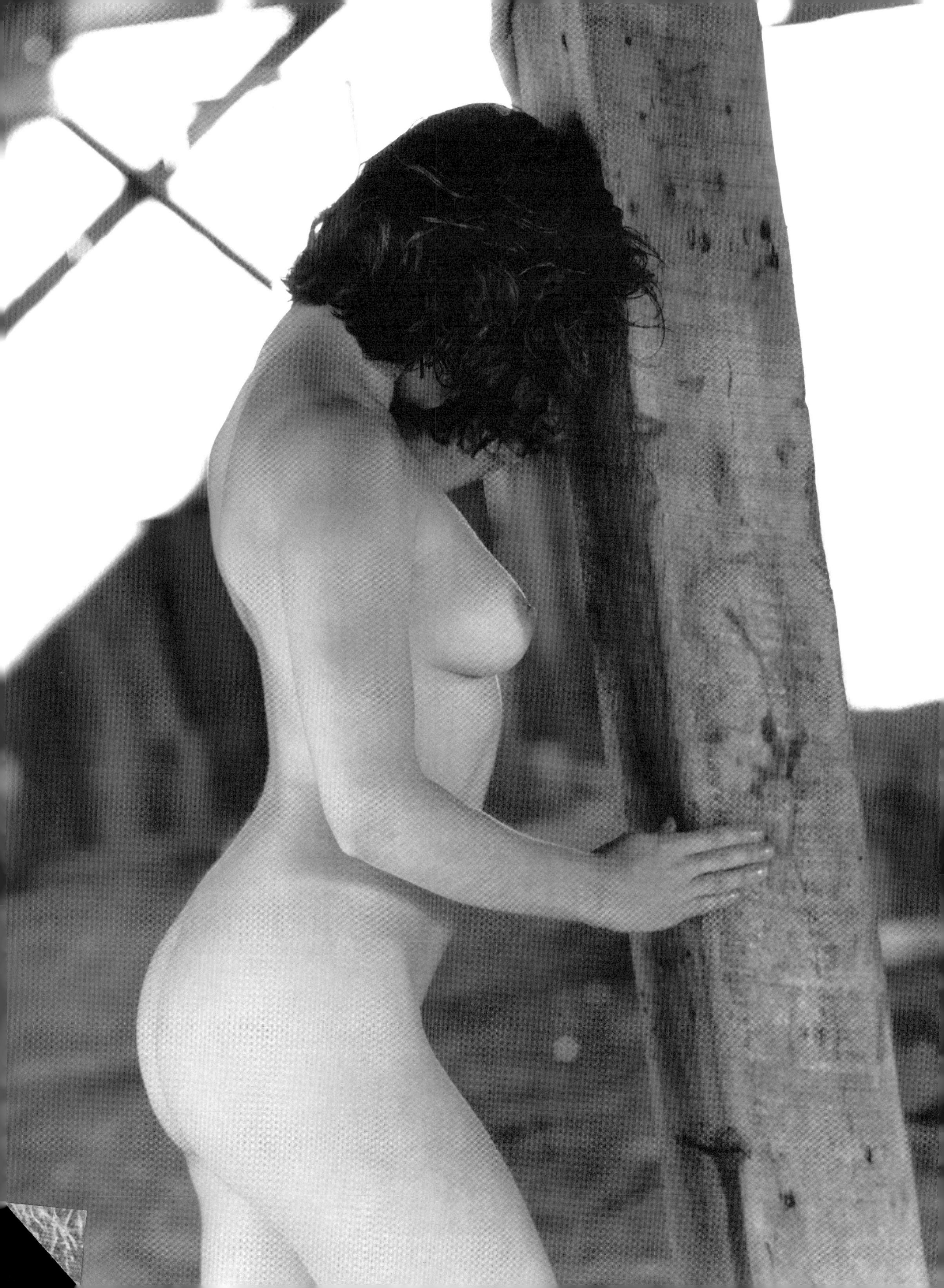

■ Posing

I usually steer away from straight-on images, since I find they don't make the body look it's best and tend to flatten out the image (especially the breasts). Shooting the body from a side view, as in this image, makes it look longer and thinner, and also tends to emphasize the model's curvature.

■ Composition

I wanted in this image to capture the sense of still and peacefulness of the barn, but also to highlight the soft texture of the model's skin and the texture of the wood. The model's face was turned slightly away from the camera to allow her hair to completely obscure it. This adds to the sense of tranquility.

■ Background

If I had this image to do over again, I would probably try to eliminate the extremely bright portions of the background which somewhat distract the viewer's eye from the model.

"Shooting the body from a side view.... makes it look longer and thinner..."

CAMERA
Hasselblad 503

LENS
150mm

FILM
Kodak TMX 100

LIGHTING
natural

EQUIPMENT
Tripod and cable release

MODEL
Jodi Bowlin

■ Posing

This model was willing to pose semi-nude, but didn't want to expose herself to the camera. Because she has a beautiful face and great legs, I decided to pose her in a way that would show off these two great features at the same time.

To make her legs look their best, I had the model stand on her toes, and point the toes of her raised leg. This tightens the legs and makes them seem even longer and thinner. To capture the beauty of her face, the model's eyes look straight into the camera, and her expression is soft and sweet.

■ Lighting

The sun positioned to the right of the camera lights the back of the model brightly, while creating a nice depth of shadow on the front of her body. A few weeds, located outside of the frame of the camera, cast interesting shadows on the model's supporting leg. Although it might be tempting to knock elements like these out of the frame, I suggest leaving them. Features like this make the image look a little less posed, and often add nice texture, as well as local points of interest to the photograph.

"To make her legs look their best, I had the model stand on her toes..."

CAMERA
Hasselblad 503

LENS
150mm

FILM
Agfapan 100

LIGHTING
natural

EQUIPMENT
tripod and cable release

MODEL
Kirsten Harrison

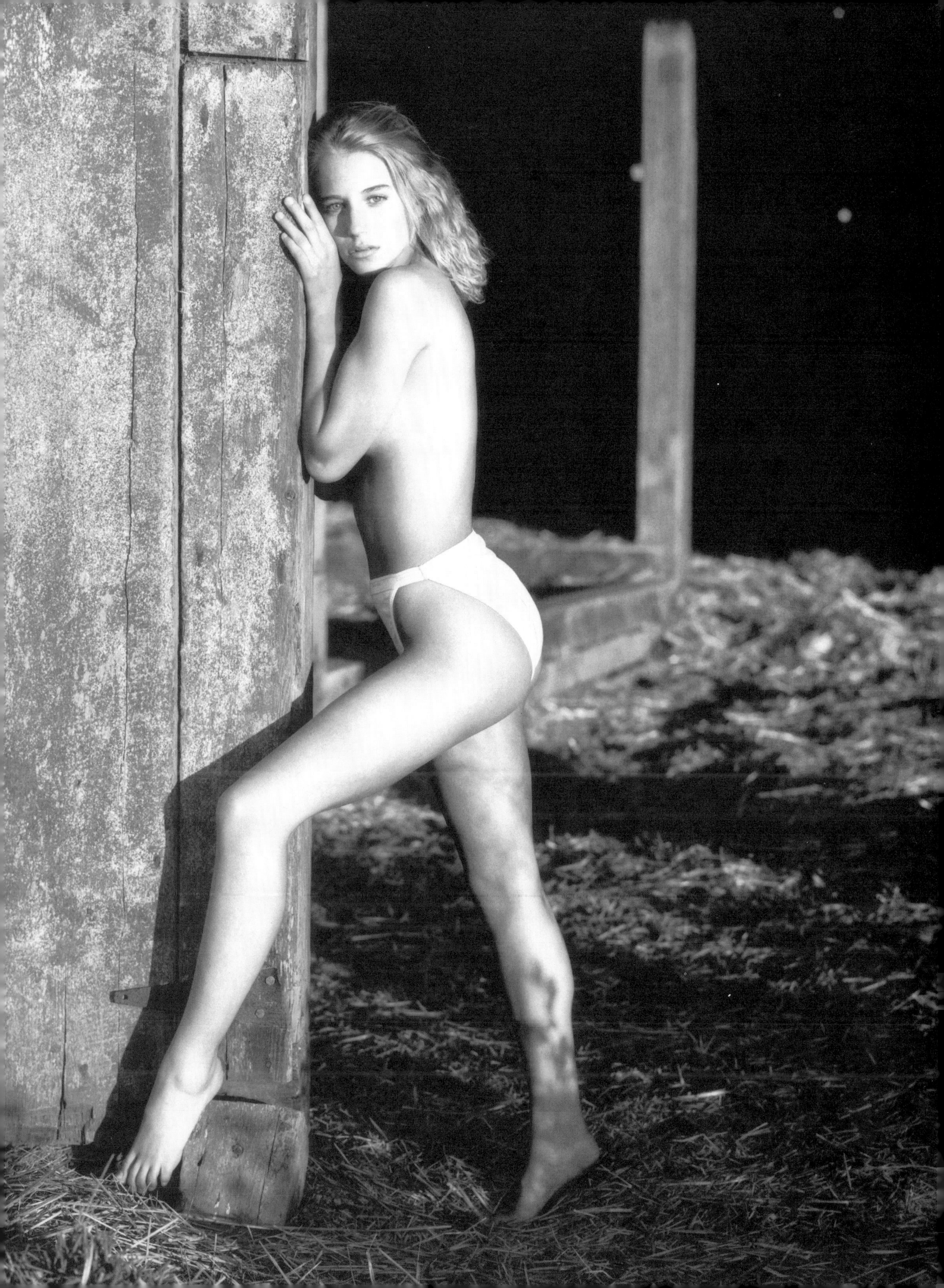

■ Pose
This model's shoulder length blonde hair and personality suggested to me an image that was rather playful. This pose and her soft, feminine, clothing, convey this idea of playfulness and sweetness very well. The pose also highlights her beautiful legs, which stand out dramatically against the darker shadows in the barn behind her.

■ Lighting
This image was shot in open shade, rather late in the day when light levels were beginning to drop. The light streaming in through the boards in the background is very soft and creates a nice sense of depth in the image, while adding a gentle glow of light behind the model.

■ Composition
Like so many of the images in this book, a strong contrast is drawn here between the soft, curvaceous form of the female body and the rigid, rough lines of nature and architecture. Here, the soft curve of the model's legs and body looks all the more feminine and attractive because of the strong, straight lines of light which form the background of the image. This compositional element reinforces the already soft feeling of the model's pose and facial expression.

"The light streaming in through the boards in the background is very soft..."

CAMERA
Hasselblad 503
LENS
150mm
FILM
Kodak TMY 400
LIGHTING
natural
EQUIPMENT
tripod and cable release
MODEL
Frankie Di

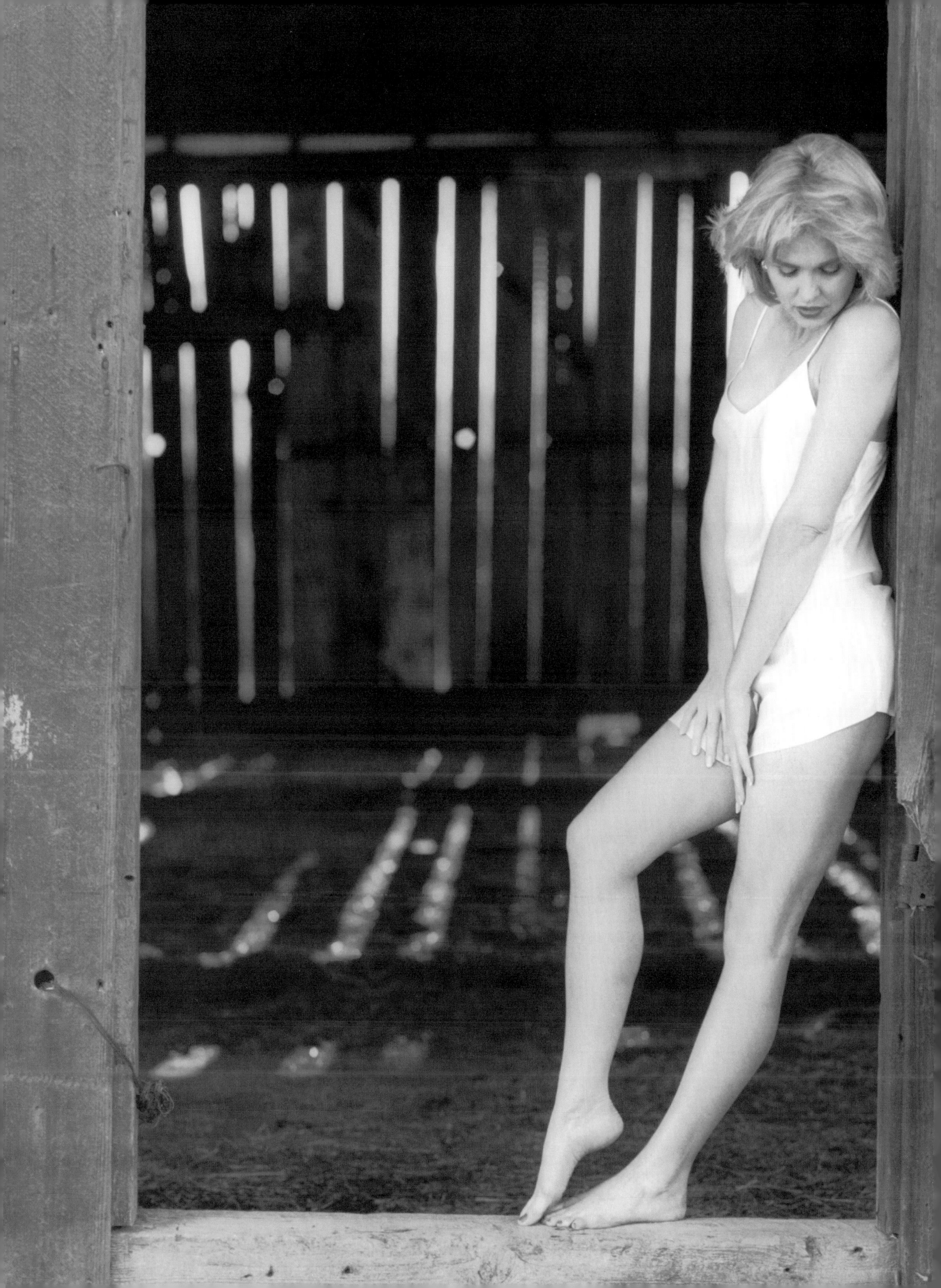

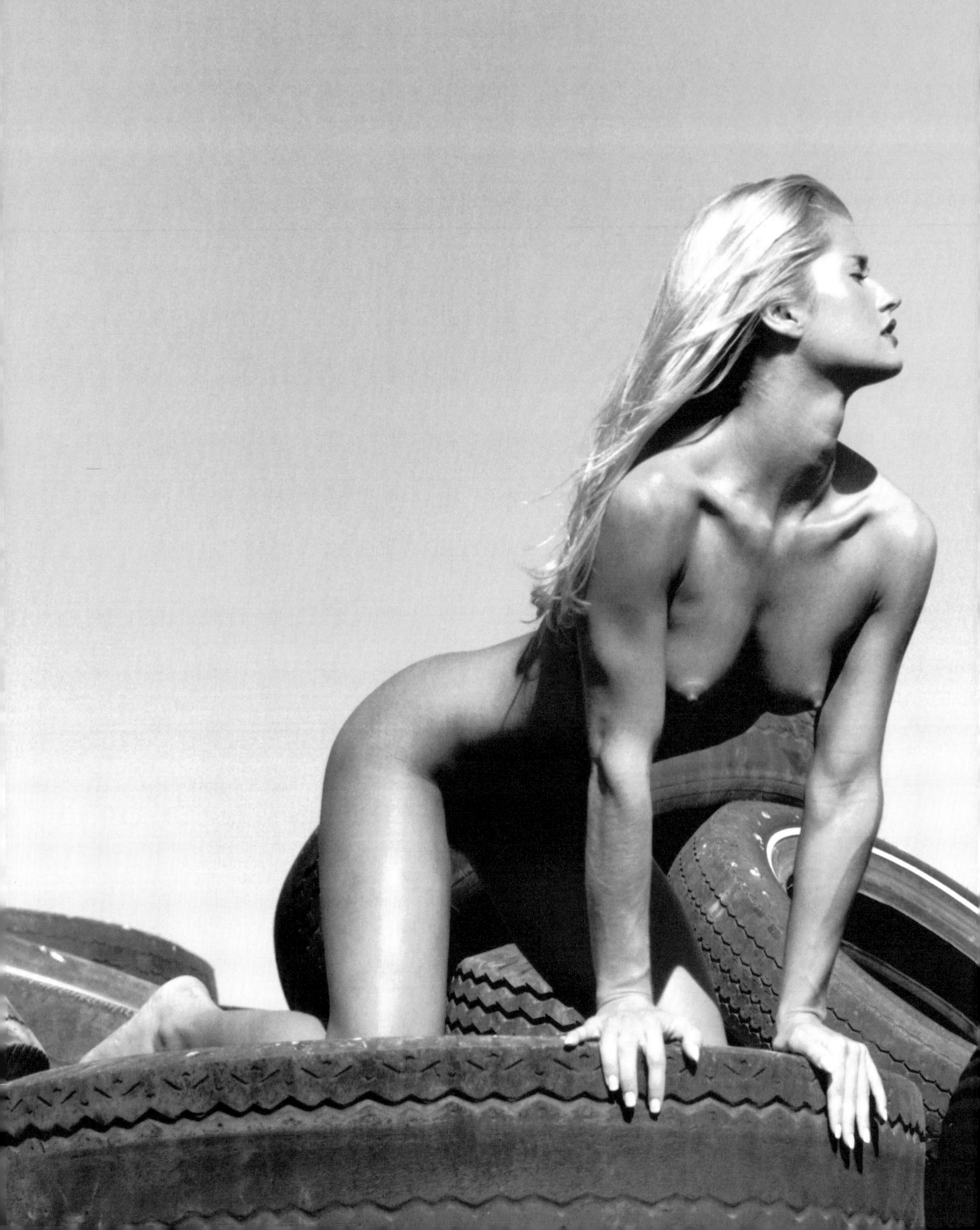

■ Photographer's Comments

Although I had envisioned this image for a long time, I had a hard time finding the right model with whom to create it. I think it was worth the wait. Many of this images in this book are the result of the same pose being tried several times with many different model's.

■ Composition

Choosing a model with very light blonde hair works well in this image, since the sky, the model's tan skin and the tires all fall into the middle to lower tonal range. This area of high local brightness (emphasized by the dramatic highlights caused by the intense sun) immediately attracts the viewer's eye to the model.

■ Lighting

A very important part of this image is the perfectly clear sky behind the model. I also wanted to shoot the image under a bright noon sun, in order to limit the amount of shadow on the face and body of the model. When shooting on location, you may have to return to the same spot repeatedly until the conditions are just right. Getting the right conditions and the right model, and having them both in the right spot at the right time takes a lot of planning, and often a little luck!

"A very important part of this image is the perfectly clear sky..."

CAMERA
Hasselblad 500CM

LENS
150mm

FILM
Kodak TMX 100

LIGHTING
natural

MODEL
Kirsten Bucheister

■ Lighting

A total of five lights were used to create the illumination in this image. The two main lights were placed in large softboxes, a third light was used on a boom above the model to light her hair. Finally, two lights are used to illuminate the background. Setting these two stops brighter than the main lights ensures the pure white background you see here.

■ Posing

This is a very flattering pose which can be shot nude without exposing anything. The soft crossing of the model's legs and hands is extremely feminine and creates nice areas of shade in the image.

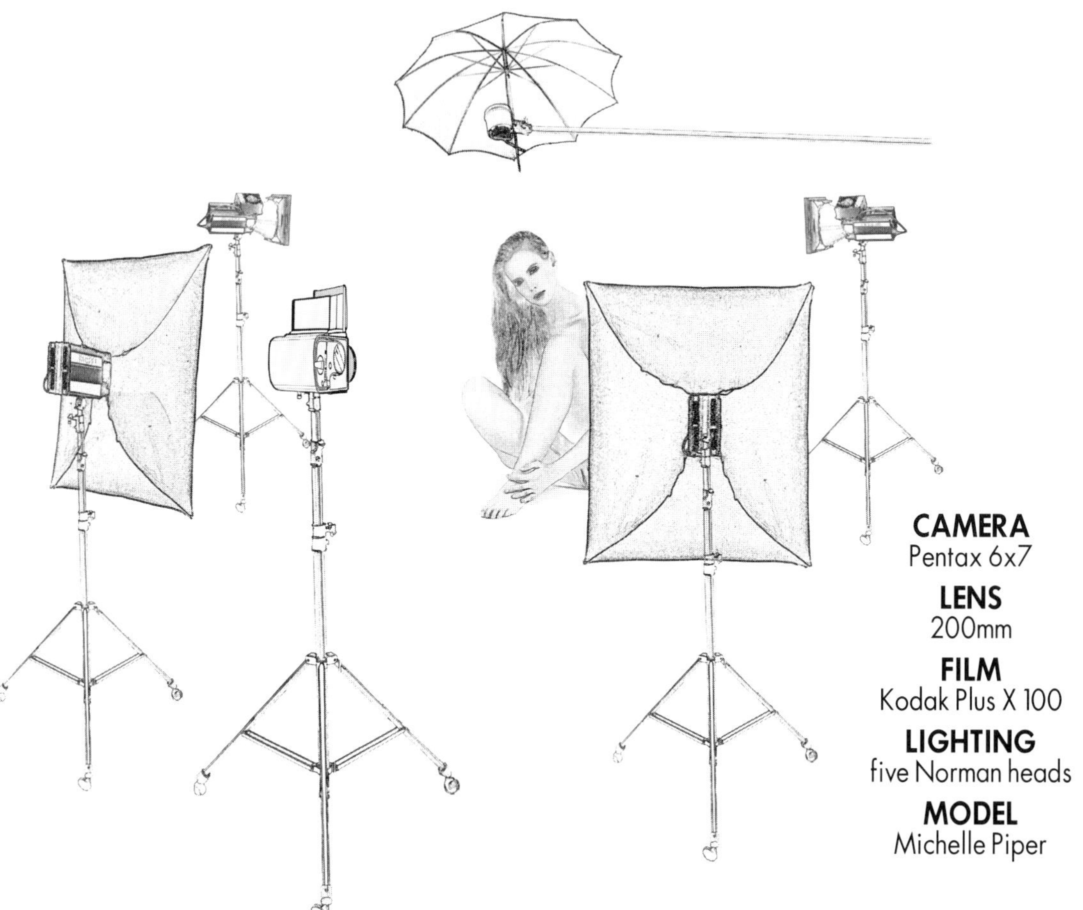

CAMERA
Pentax 6x7

LENS
200mm

FILM
Kodak Plus X 100

LIGHTING
five Norman heads

MODEL
Michelle Piper

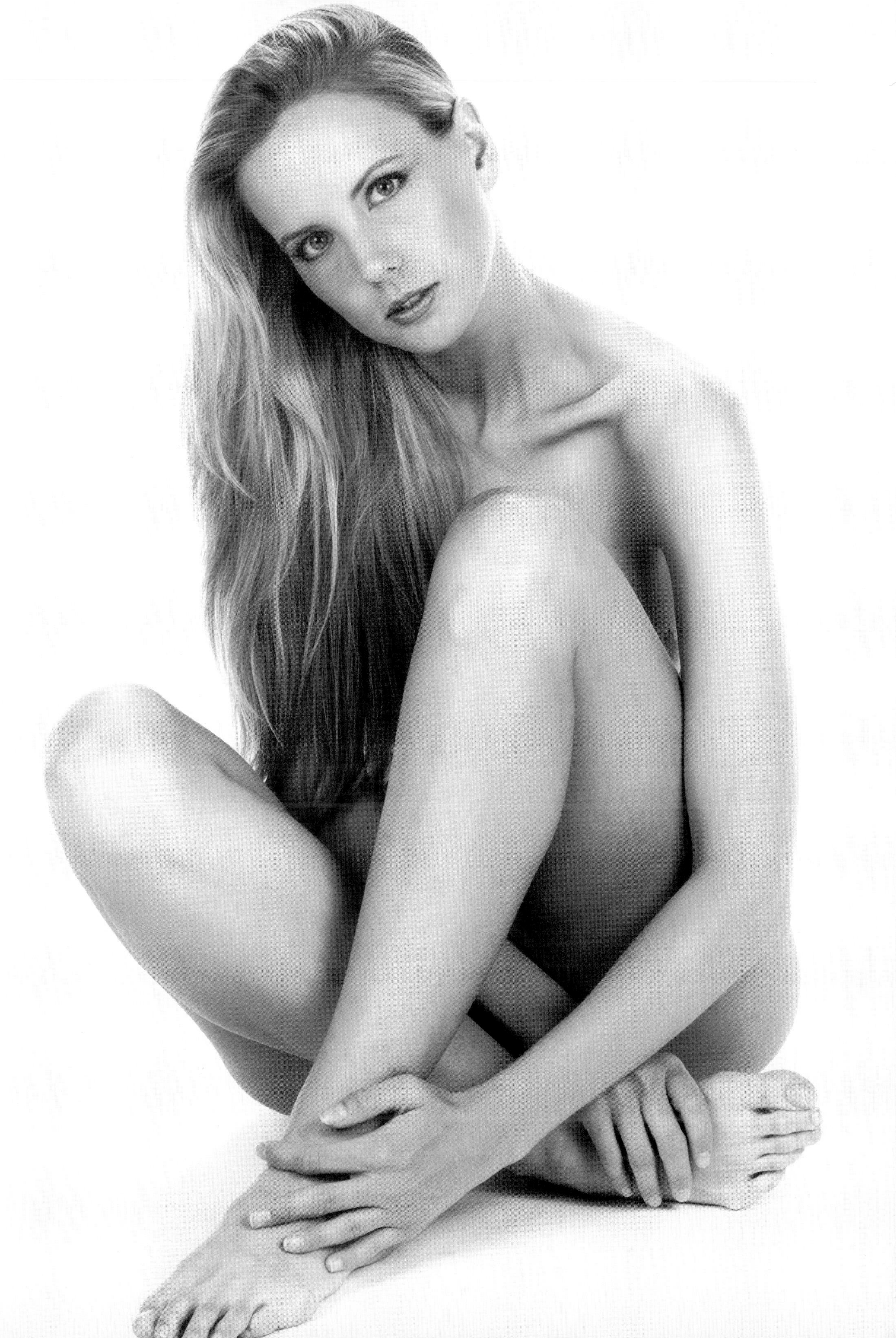

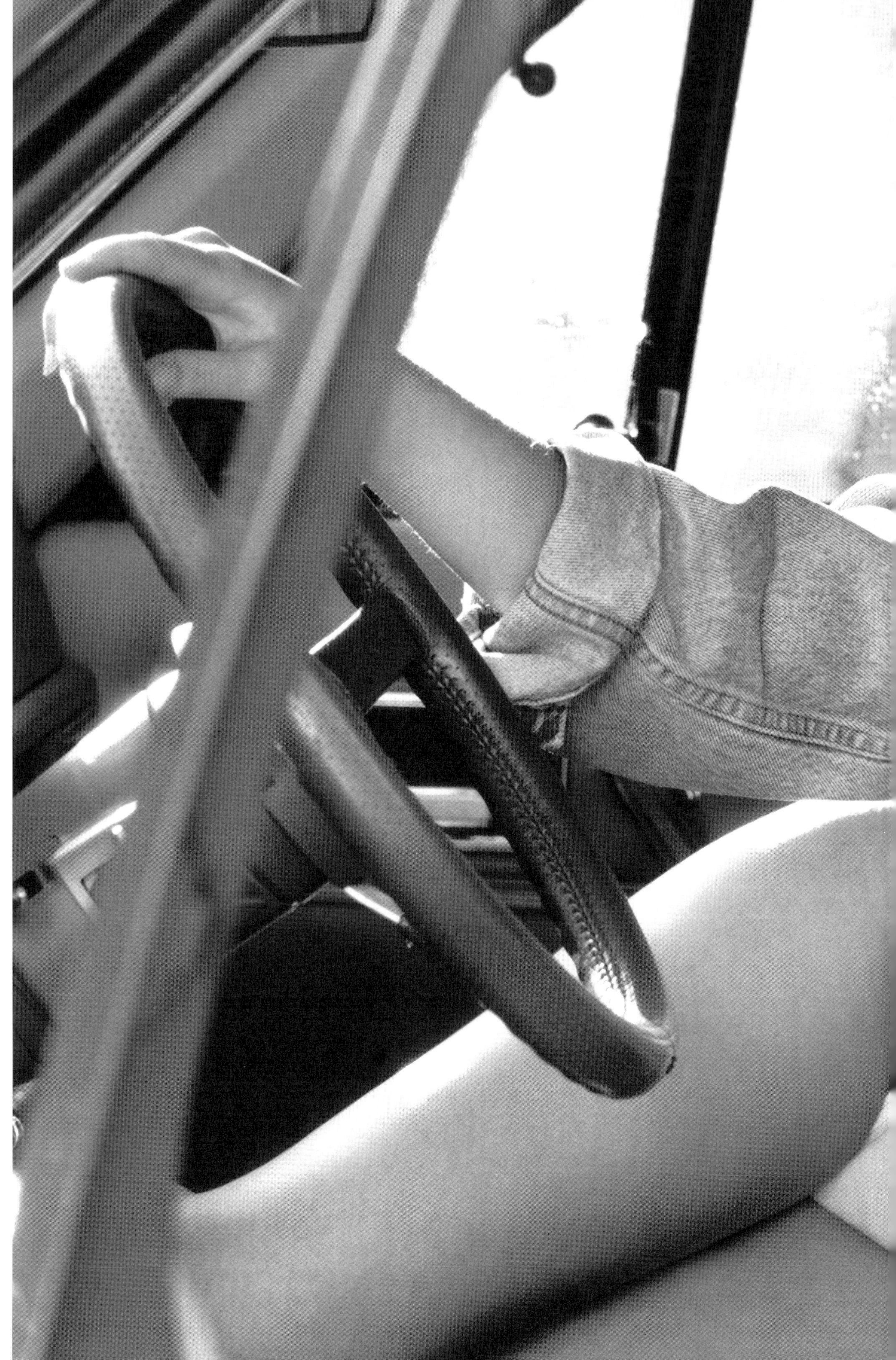

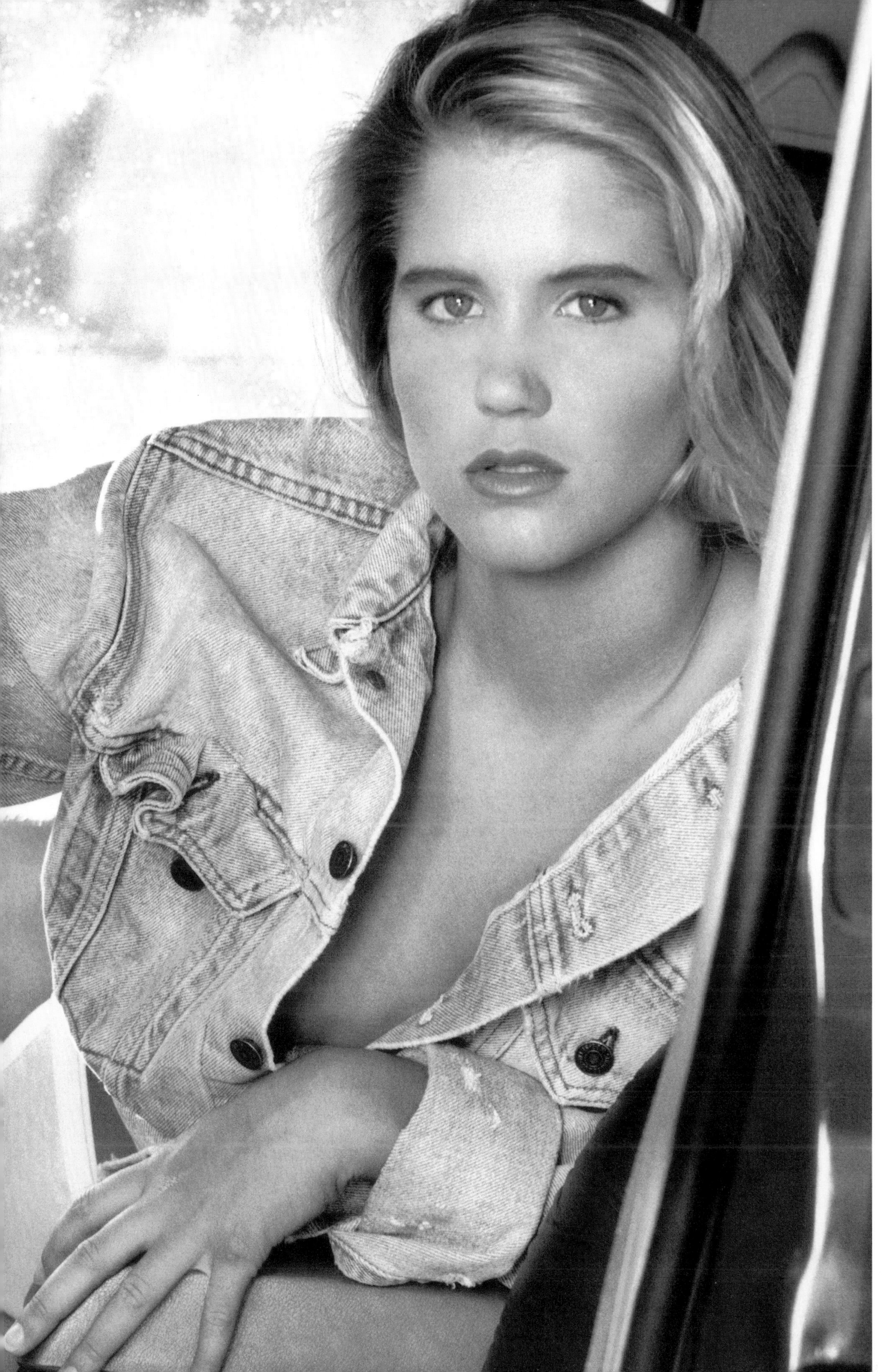

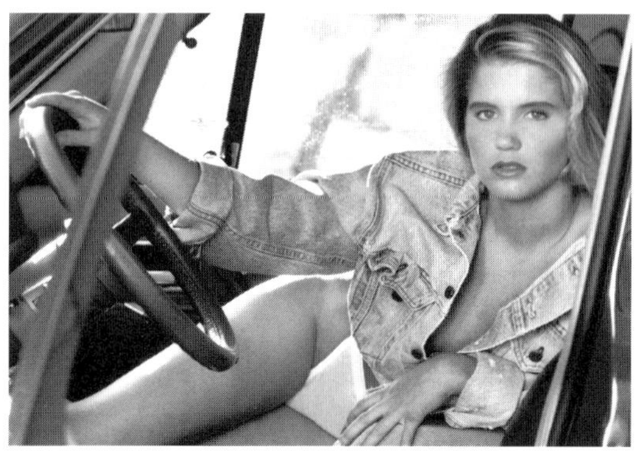

■ Film

Film selection is an individual choice. I selected Kodak TMY 400 here because I was looking for depth of field and sharpness. (Notice that the model's hands are both in almost identical focus, despite the fact that her right hand is well in the foreground.) Shooting test rolls is the only way to find out what will work best for you.

■ Windows

Objects seen through the window behind the model could have been a concern, but this problem is easily solved by misting the windows with a mixture of water and glycerine. This also helps to diffuse the light coming in through the window.

■ Reflectors

Although the light in this photograph was natural, the late afternoon sun was behind the model when the photo was shot. Therefore, the placement of a silver reflector was crucial to getting light inside the car and onto the model's face. The light from the window behind her still catches her thigh and right hand, but the reflector balances this with a soft light on the front of the model.

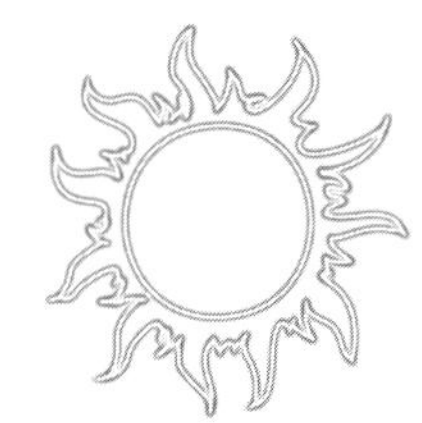

CAMERA
Hasselblad 503

LENS
150mm

FILM
Kodak TMY 400

LIGHTING
natural light, reflector

MODEL
Heather Larson

Index

Other Books from Amherst Media, Inc.

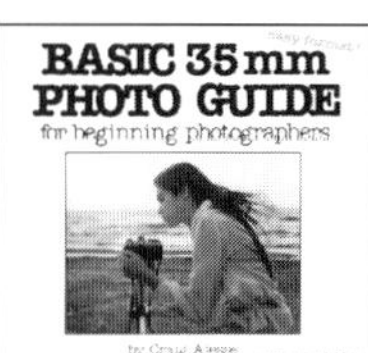

Basic 35mm Photo Guide

Craig Alesse

Great for beginning photographers! Designed to teach 35mm basics step-by-step — completely illustrated. Features the latest cameras. Includes: 35mm automatic and semi-automatic cameras, camera handling, *f*-stops, shutter speeds, and more! $12.95 list, 9x8, 112p, 178 photos, order no. 1051.

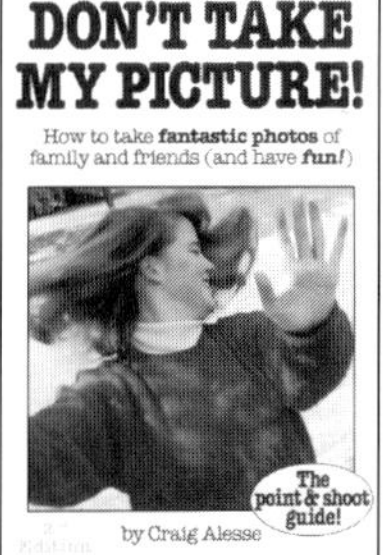

Don't Take My Picture

Craig Alesse

This is the second edition of the fun-to-read guide to taking fantastic photos of family and friends. Best selling author, Craig Alesse, shows you in clear, simple language how to shoot pictures, work with light, and capture the moment. Make everyone in your pictures look their best! $9.95 list, 6x9, 104p, 100+ photos, order no. 1099.

Build Your Own Home Darkroom

Lista Duren & Will McDonald

This classic book shows how to build a high quality, inexpensive darkroom in your basement, spare room, or almost anywhere. Information on: darkroom design, woodworking, tools, and more! $17.95 list, 8½x11, 160p, order no. 1092.

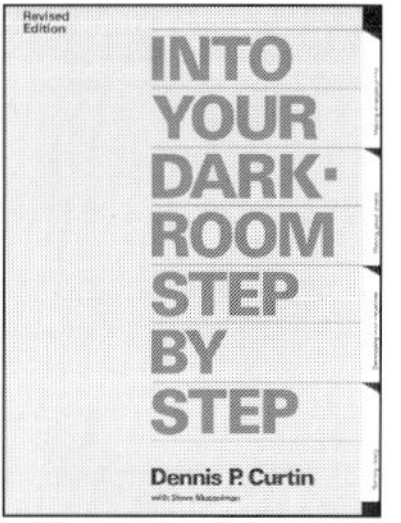

Into Your Darkroom Step-by-Step

Dennis P. Curtin

The ideal beginning darkroom guide. Easy to follow and fully illustrated each step of the way. Information on: equipment you'll need, set-up, making proof sheets and much more! $17.95 list, 8½x11, 90p, hundreds of photos, order no. 1093.

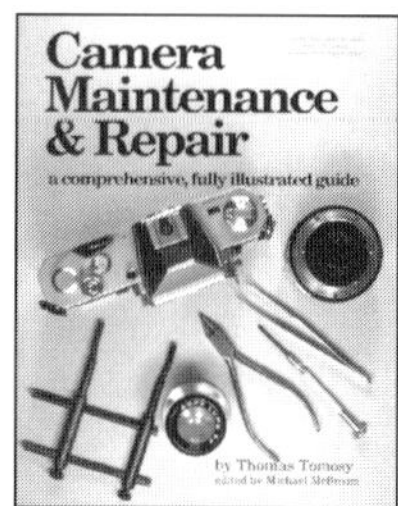

Camera Maintenance & Repair

Thomas Tomosy

A step-by-step, fully illustrated guide by a master camera repair technician. Sections include: testing camera functions, general maintenance, basic tools needed, basic repairs for accessories, camera electronics, plus "quick tips" for maintenance and more! $24.95 list, 8½x11, 176p, order no. 1158.

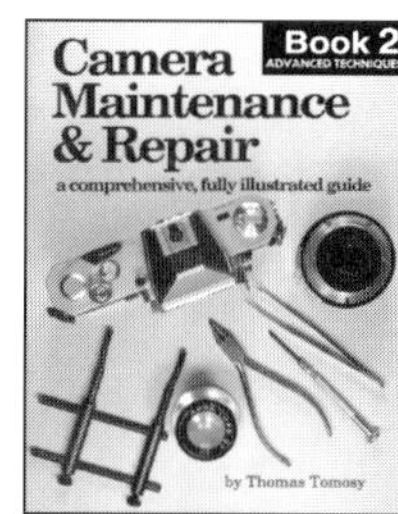

Camera Maintenance & Repair Book 2

Thomas Tomosy

Advanced troubleshooting and repair building on the basics covered in the first book. Includes; mechanical and electronic SLRs, zoom lenses, medium format, troubleshooting, repairing plastic and metal parts, and more. $29.95 list, 8½x11, 176p, 150+ photos, charts, tables, appendices, index, glossary, order no. 1558.

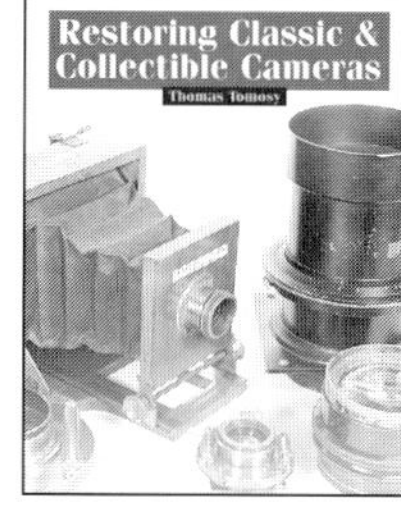

Restoring Classic & Collectible Cameras

Thomas Tomosy

A must for camera buffs and collectors! Clear, step-by-step instructions show how to restore a classic or vintage camera. Work on leather, brass and wood to restore your valuable collectibles. $34.95 list, 8½x11, 128p, b&w photos and illustrations, glossary, index, order no. 1613.

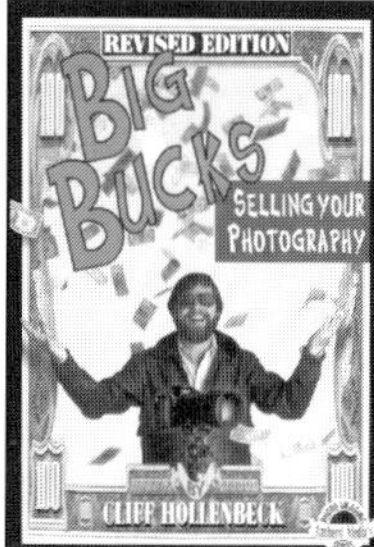

Big Bucks Selling Your Photography

Cliff Hollenbeck

A complete photo business package for all photographers. Includes secrets to making big bucks, starting up, getting paid the right price, and creating successful portfolios! Features setting financial, marketing and creative goals. This book will help to organize business planning, bookkeeping, and taxes. $15.95 list, 6x9, 336p, order no. 1177.

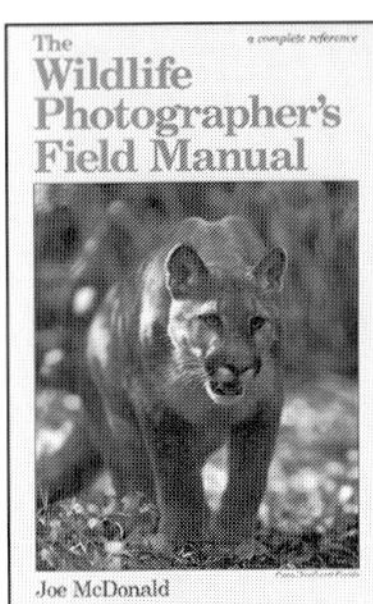

The Wildlife Photographer's Field Manual

Joe McDonald

The complete reference for every wildlife photographer. A practical, comprehensive, easy-to-read guide with useful information, including: the right equipment and accessories, field shooting, lighting, focusing techniques, and more! Features special sections on insects, reptiles, birds, mammals and more! $14.95 list, 6x9, 200p, order no. 1005.

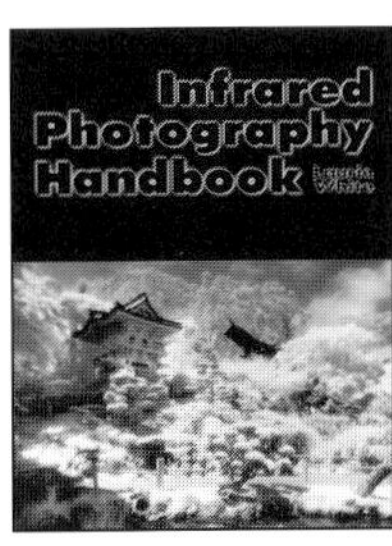

Infrared Photography Handbook

Laurie White

Covers black and white infrared photography: focus, lenses, film loading, film speed rating, heat sensitivity, batch testing, paper stocks, and filters. Black & white photos illustrate how IR film reacts in portrait, landscape, and architectural photography. $24.95 list, 8½x11, 104p, 50 b&w photos, charts & diagrams, order no. 1419.

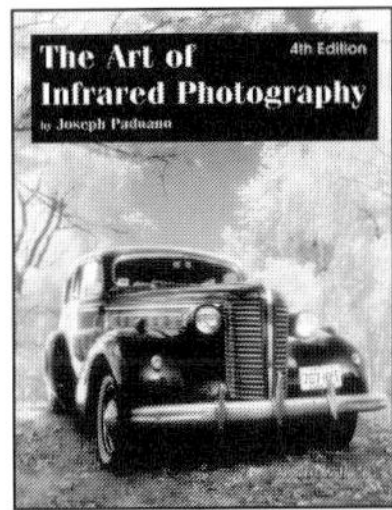

The Art of Infrared Photography / 4th Edition

Joe Paduano

A practical, comprehensive guide to the art of infrared photography. Tells what to expect and how to control results. Includes: anticipating effects, color infrared, digital infrared, using filters, focusing, developing, printing, handcoloring, toning, and more! $29.95 list, 8½x11, 112p, order no. 1052.

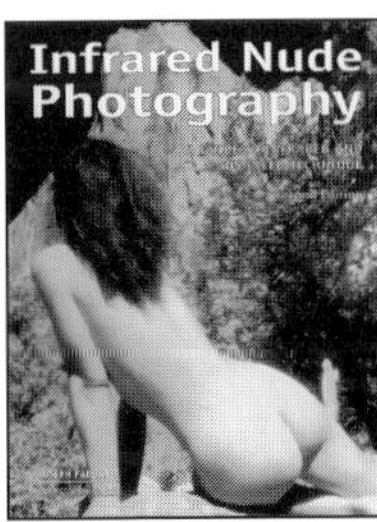

Infrared Nude Photography

Joseph Paduano

A stunning collection of images with informative how-to text. Over 50 infrared photos presented as a portfolio of classic nude work. Shot on location in natural settings, including the Grand Canyon, Bryce Canyon and the New Jersey Shore. $29.95 list, 8½x11, 96p, over 50 photos, order no. 1080.

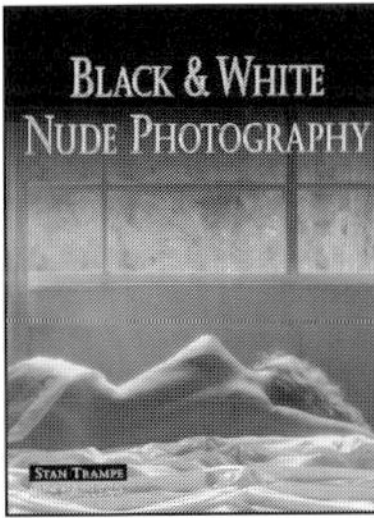

Black & White Nude Photography

Stan Trampe

This book teaches the essentials for beginning fine art nude photography. Includes info on finding your first models, selecting equipment, scenarios of a typical shoot, and more! Includes 60 photos taken with b&w and infrared films. $24.95 list, 8½x11, 112p, index, order no. 1592.

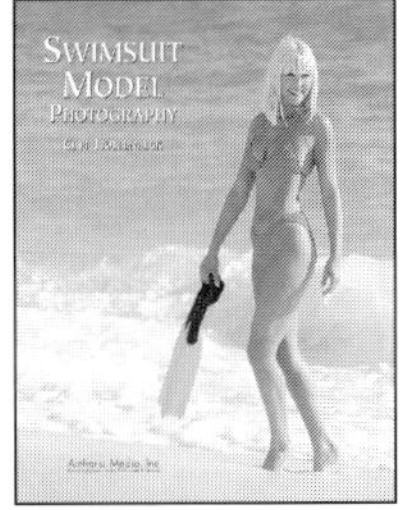

Swimsuit Model Photography

Cliff Hollenbeck

A complete guide to swimsuit model photography. Includes: finding and working with models, selecting equipment, posing, props, backgrounds, and much more! By the author of *Big Bucks Selling Your Photography* and *Great Travel Photography*. $29.95 list, 8½x11, 112p, over 100 b&w and color photos, index, order no. 1605.

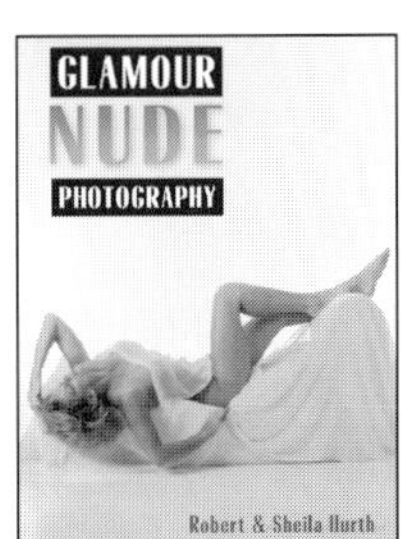

Glamour Nude Photography

Robert and Sheila Hurth

Create stunning nude images! Robert and Sheila Hurth guide you through selecting a subject, choosing locations, lighting, and shooting techniques. Includes information on posing, equipment, makeup and hair styles, and much more! $24.95 list, 8½x11, 144p, over 100 b&w and color photos, index, order no. 1499.

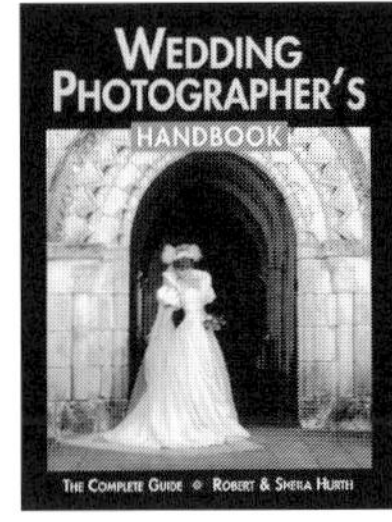

Wedding Photographer's Handbook

Robert and Sheila Hurth

The complete step-by-step guide to succeeding in the exciting and profitable world of wedding photography. Packed with shooting tips, equipment lists, must-get photo lists, business strategies, and much more! $24.95 list, 8½x11, 176p, index, b&w and color photos, diagrams, order no. 1485.

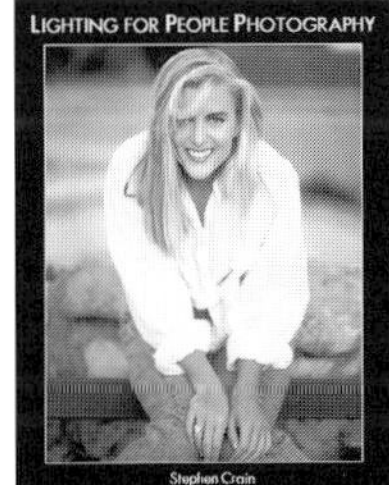

Lighting for People Photography

Stephen Crain

The complete guide to lighting. Includes: set-ups, equipment information, how to control strobe and natural lighting, and much more! Features diagrams, illustrations, and exercises for practicing the lighting techniques discussed in each chapter. $29.95 list, 8½x11, 112p, b&w and color photos, glossary, index, order no. 1296.

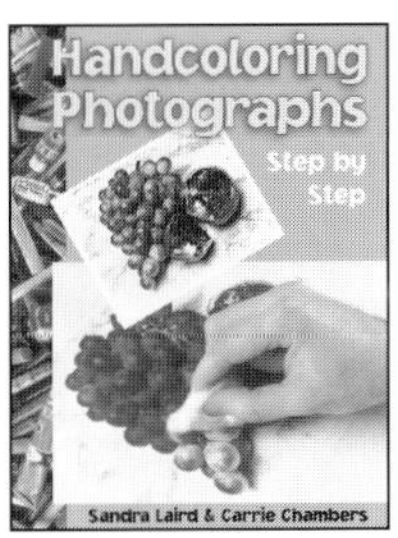

Handcoloring Photographs Step-by-Step

Sandra Laird & Carey Chambers

Learn to handcolor photographs step-by-step with the new standard handcoloring reference. Covers a variety of coloring media. Includes colorful photographic examples. $29.95 list, 8½x11, 112p, 100+ color and b&w photos, order no. 1543.